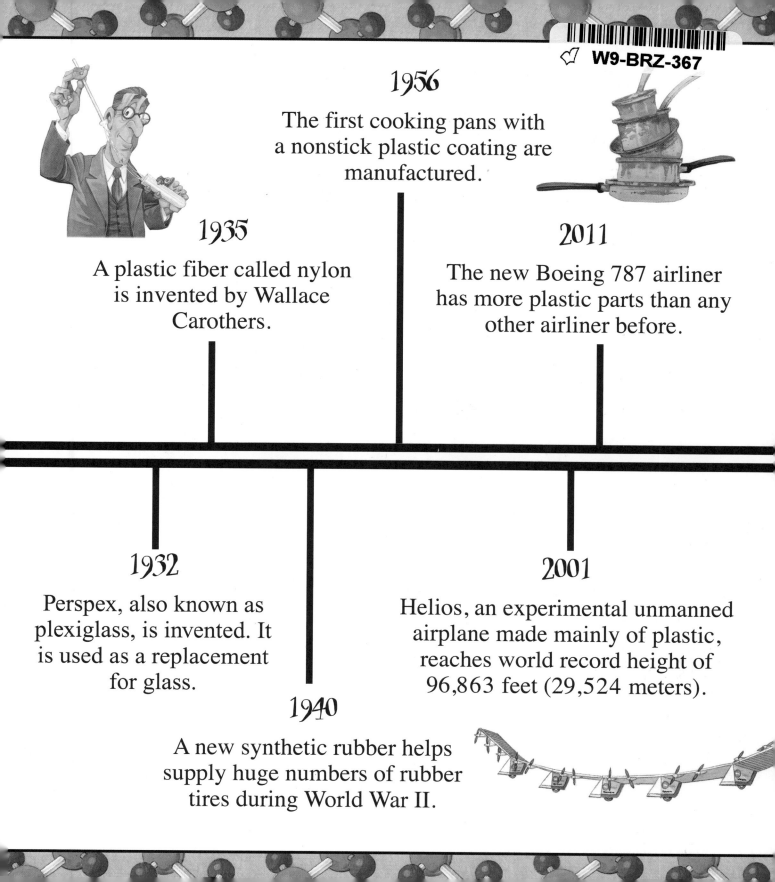

W9-BRZ-367

1956

The first cooking pans with a nonstick plastic coating are manufactured.

1935

A plastic fiber called nylon is invented by Wallace Carothers.

2011

The new Boeing 787 airliner has more plastic parts than any other airliner before.

1932

Perspex, also known as plexiglass, is invented. It is used as a replacement for glass.

2001

Helios, an experimental unmanned airplane made mainly of plastic, reaches world record height of 96,863 feet (29,524 meters).

1940

A new synthetic rubber helps supply huge numbers of rubber tires during World War II.

What Is Plastic?

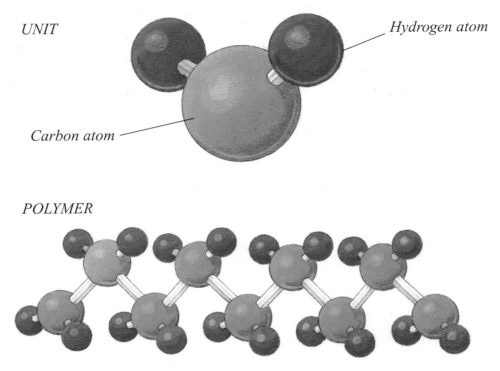

UNIT

Hydrogen atom

Carbon atom

POLYMER

Plastic is a material such as nylon, PVC, or polythene that can be molded into a new shape while it is soft. It then sets, keeping its new shape. The word *plastic* comes from the Greek word *plastikos*, meaning "able to be molded or shaped."

Everything you can see and touch is made of invisibly tiny particles called atoms. They're so small that you can't see them, no matter how good your eyesight is. Atoms often join together in small groups called molecules. Most molecules contain just a few atoms. Plastic is different. It's made of very long molecules. Each molecule looks like a length of bicycle chain. It has hundreds or thousands of identical units joined together to form a long chain called a polymer. These long chains can slide over each other, making the plastic soft and easily shaped when it is hot, and then they link together when it cools, locking in the new plastic shape.

Author:

Ian Graham earned a degree in applied physics at City University, London. He then took a graduate diploma in journalism. Since becoming a freelance author and journalist, he has written more than 250 children's nonfiction books.

Artist:

David Antram was born in Brighton, England, in 1958. He studied at Eastbourne College of Art and then worked in advertising for 15 years before becoming a full-time artist. He has illustrated many children's nonfiction books.

Series creator:

David Salariya was born in Dundee, Scotland. He has illustrated a wide range of books and has created and designed many new series for publishers in the UK and overseas. David established The Salariya Book Company in 1989. He lives in Brighton, England, with his wife, illustrator Shirley Willis, and their son, Jonathan.

Editor: Caroline Coleman

Editorial Assistant: Mark Williams

PAPER FROM SUSTAINABLE FORESTS

© The Salariya Book Company Ltd MMXVI
No part of this publication may be reproduced in whole or in part, or stored in a retrieval system, or transmitted in any form or by any means, electronic, mechanical, photocopying, recording, or otherwise, without written permission of the publisher. For information regarding permission, write to the copyright holder.

Published in Great Britain in 2016 by
The Salariya Book Company Ltd
25 Marlborough Place, Brighton BN1 1UB

ISBN-13: 978-0-531-21929-4 (lib. bdg.) 978-0-531-22053-5 (pbk.)

All rights reserved.
Published in 2016 in the United States
by Franklin Watts
An imprint of Scholastic Inc.
Published simultaneously in Canada.

A CIP catalog record for this book is available
from the Library of Congress.

Printed and bound in China.
Printed on paper from sustainable sources.
1 2 3 4 5 6 7 8 9 10 R 25 24 23 22 21 20 19 18 17 16

SCHOLASTIC, FRANKLIN WATTS, and associated logos are trademarks and/or registered trademarks of Scholastic Inc.

This book is sold subject to the conditions that it shall not, by way of trade or otherwise, be lent, resold, hired out, or otherwise circulated without the publisher's prior consent in any form or binding or cover other than that in which it is published and without similar condition being imposed on the subsequent purchaser.

You Wouldn't Want to Live Without™
Plastic!

Written by
Ian Graham

Illustrated by
David Antram

Series created by
David Salariya

Franklin Watts®
An Imprint of Scholastic Inc.

Contents

Introduction

Look around your home or school and you'll see plastic everywhere. It's in your computer, cell phone, television set, toys, games, pens, sports equipment, and even the books you read. Your clothes, carpets, furniture, and even the paint on your walls probably contain plastic, too. Look in your kitchen. You'll find a lot of plastic there. Plastic plays such an important part in everyone's life today that it's difficult to imagine what the world would be like without it. Many of the things you do every day would be different, or more difficult, or maybe even impossible if plastic had never been invented. And many of the things you buy would be much more expensive without it. You really wouldn't want to live without plastic.

A World Without Plastic?

HOPE YOU LIKE BAGGY CLOTHES! Without plastic, the synthetic fibers that give modern clothes their stretchiness would not exist.

Today, so many of the things we use either are made of plastic or have some plastic parts. There are lots of different types of plastic. Some are soft, others are hard. Some are see-through, others aren't. Some are smooth and glossy, others are dull and rough. And plastic items can be made in white, black, and every color of the rainbow. The story was very different just over a hundred years ago. The many different types of plastic we have today hadn't been invented yet. Can you imagine what it would be like if plastic had never been invented? We might not have things like cell phones, computers, or the Internet.

BEFORE PLASTIC, glue was often made by boiling up animal hooves and hides. Most modern glues contain some form of plastic.

WITHOUT PLASTIC, you probably wouldn't have computers, cell phones, or game consoles, because so many of their parts are made of plastic.

PLASTIC FURNITURE can be made in almost any shape. Some shapes would be difficult to make as easily or cheaply from other materials. Some couldn't be made at all.

A home without plastic

Horse hooves were used to make glue because they contain keratin (as do your fingernails!). When hooves are melted in boiling water and acid is added, the keratin melts and forms thick, jelly-like glue.

Wool

Cotton

Brass

Paper

Cotton

Cotton

Wood

Wool

Glass

Leather

Wood

Wood

Before Plastic

Plastic was not common in people's homes until the 1950s. Before then, nearly everything is made of traditional materials such as wood, metal, stone, glass, leather, and natural fibers. Small items like buttons and knife handles are made from ivory, horn, and antler. These materials have been used for thousands of years. They have to be collected from wherever they can be found in nature and then processed to change them into useful things. The people who process them have years of experience in working with natural materials. They know about each material's strengths and weaknesses. However, plastic is about to change all of this.

Wood for building

Wool for making clothes

PIANO KEYS used to be made of ivory from elephant tusks. Playing a piano was known as "tickling the ivories." Ivory from one tusk could make 45 keyboards.

BEFORE COMBS were made of plastic, they were made of bone or antler. Their teeth were brittle and often snapped off. Plastic combs have flexible teeth that last longer.

Antler for making tools

You Can Do It!

Clothes have care labels that tell you which fabrics the clothes are made of and how they should be cleaned. Can you find these labels in your clothes?

Bone for making tools

Animal skin for making clothes

SHRINKING can be a problem when washing clothes made of natural fibers, especially woolen items. Clothes with synthetic fibers can endure repeated washing.

SITTING PRETTY.
Cushions, chairs, and soft toys used to be stuffed with straw, wool, wood shavings, sawdust, feathers, and horsehair. Today plastic fibers and foam are used.

The First Plastics

The first plastics are made from natural materials. One of the strangest is shellac. It is made from a substance called lac, which is produced by an insect, the lac bug. About 100,000 lac bugs produce 1 pound (500 grams) of shellac. Shellac can be molded to form all kinds of different shapes. The first sound recordings in the early 1900s are on records made of shellac. Another early plastic is Parkesine, patented in 1856 by Alexander Parkes. Parkesine is made from cellulose, a substance that comes from plants. The first photographic film is made from long strips of a clear plastic called celluloid, patented in 1870. One plastic is even made from milk! If modern plastics had not been created, we might still be using plastics made from natural materials.

SHELLAC RECORDS are very popular, but very brittle. Many of them end up cracked and broken. Plastic vinyl discs introduced in the 1930s are not so brittle, so they last much longer. They quickly replace shellac discs.

THE LAC BUG produces a red liquid called lac, which hardens on tree branches to form a glassy red material. It is collected, purified, and processed to make shellac.

Thank you!

It's shellac, from little bugs!

You Can Do It!

Ask an adult to heat a cup of milk.* Don't let it boil. Add two tablespoons of clear vinegar. Stir until lumps appear. When cool, squish them together. You've made milk plastic!

*SAFETY: Be very careful not to splash or spill hot milk!

THE FIRST PHOTOGRAPHS are made one by one, on metal plates or sheets of glass. Celluloid film makes it possible to take photographs quickly enough to produce the first movies.

BRITISH QUEEN MARY (1867–1953) owns plastic jewelry made from milk! Milk contains a substance called casein. This is processed to make plastic called casein plastic or Galalith.

11

Science to the Rescue!

In the early 1900s, scientists start looking for new ways to make plastics. Instead of processing natural materials, they combine chemicals to make new ones. These plastics, created by scientists in laboratories, are called synthetic plastics. The first synthetic plastic in 1907 is named Bakelite after its inventor, Leo Baekeland. By the 1920s, radios, cameras, jewelry, light switches, electrical plugs, and clocks are being made from Bakelite. In the 1930s, Wallace Carothers creates a famous plastic called nylon, which is still in use today.

SHIRTS MADE OF NYLON are popular, but not for long. Electric charges build up on the fibers and give you an electric shock when you touch something metal, like a door handle. Ouch!

New Uses for Plastic

BAKELITE ARRIVES just as an invention called radio becomes popular. Millions of Bakelite radios are sold from 1920 to 1950, before television becomes widely available.

SO MANY THINGS are made of Bakelite that it becomes known as "the material of a thousand uses." You can even have a coffin made of Bakelite!

SOME PLASTICS created in the early 1900s are still used today. Look inside any small machine and you'll probably find gearwheels and other parts made of nylon.

WALLACE CAROTHERS (1896–1937) was an American chemist credited with the invention of nylon.

Wallace Carothers

Nylon fibers

13

Top Tip

Nylon is used for making gearwheels because they're quieter than metal gearwheels, they don't need to be oiled, they don't rust, and they last longer.

Plastics Take Off

During World War II (1939–1945), all sorts of materials are in short supply, including rubber. Scientists are given the job of creating a new material that can be used instead of natural rubber. They succeed in making a stretchy rubberlike plastic. They manufacture other new plastics, too, such as Kodel, Terylene, and Dacron. After the war, millions of people are rebuilding their lives in new homes. Factories start making all the products they need, using the new plastics created in the 1930s and 1940s. It is around this time that plastic bottles begin to replace glass bottles. Plastics really take off.

THERE ISN'T ENOUGH natural rubber to make tires and other rubber parts for all the trucks, planes, and machines used during World War II. Scientists create synthetic rubber to solve the problem.

IN THE 1930s, a new see-through plastic called Perspex (plexiglass) is used to make cockpit canopies of fighter planes. Bulletproof glass is also made by placing plastic between two sheets of glass.

DANGER! Before bottles were made of plastic, they were made of thick, heavy glass. These bottles shatter if they are dropped or knocked over. Plastic bottles are much safer—they bounce!

You Can Do It!

Are any parts of your toys not made of plastic? Why do you think they aren't plastic? They might have to be stronger, harder, or springier than the plastic parts. Or is there another reason?

MORE DANGER! Playing with toys wouldn't be so safe if plastic had not been invented. Toys were once made of tinplate and lead. Tinplate has sharp edges and lead is poisonous.

Ouch!

Into the Space Age

Mass-produced plastic products reach shops in the 1950s just as the first spaceflights hit the headlines. Plastic is a space-age material for a space-age world. After the dark days of World War II, plastic makes everyone feel that the future has arrived. The first plastic products break more easily than sturdy wood and metal products, and they can't be repaired as easily, but it doesn't matter because new plastic products are less expensive. It's the beginning of our "throwaway" lifestyle. Instead of repairing something, we throw it away and buy something new to replace it.

A PLASTIC HOOP called a hula hoop is a must-have toy in the late 1950s. The idea is to spin it around your waist and keep it going by swiveling your hips.

THE FIRST TRANSISTOR RADIOS, made of plastic, appear in the 1950s. Their sound quality isn't great, but they are very popular among young people, because they are so small and portable.

You Can Do It!

Mix one tablespoon of cornstarch with one tablespoon of water. Stir in a tablespoon of white craft glue (this contains plastic polymer.) Let it set and it will turn into plastic slime.

BEFORE THE 1960s, dolls' heads were often made of china or porcelain. They broke very easily, so they had to be handled carefully. Plastic dolls are much tougher, so they last longer.

THE FIRST MODERN CREDIT CARDS are issued in the United States in the 1950s. These plastic cards make it easier for people to buy new products from stores.

17

It's a Plastic World!

STICK WITH IT. Many of the glues used today, from craft glue to superglue, contain plastic polymers. As the glue sets, its long polymer chains lock together.

There are thousands of different plastics for making all sorts of products. Think of all the gadgets you enjoy using. Your game console, laptop, tablet computer, and headphones all depend on plastic. Many of them have plastic cases, buttons, and switches. The electronic circuits inside them depend on plastic, too. The circuits are built on circuit boards made of plastic. Their microchips are sealed in plastic blocks. All kinds of electrical equipment, from table lamps to vacuum cleaners, work safely because of plastic. Their electrical wiring is covered with plastic to stop electric currents from escaping. Without plastic, life would be truly shocking. ZAP!

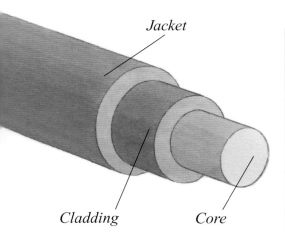

Jacket

Cladding   *Core*

LIGHT PIPES. The cables that carry telephone calls and computer information were once made of metal. Now, many of them are made of thin strands of glass or plastic called optical fibers.

THE GLOSSY PAPER used for printing photographs and magazine covers is coated with plastic to make it supersmooth and shiny. The coating is also designed to help colored ink stick to the paper.

PARACHUTES, yacht sails, and hot-air balloons are made of a very strong plastic fabric called ripstop. Its fibers are woven together to make a fabric that will not rip or tear easily.

ULTRALIGHTWEIGHT PLASTIC has made it possible to build aircraft that were impossible to make in the past. Helios was an electric plane powered by the energy in sunlight.

How It Works

Plastic circuit boards are covered with metal tracks. The tracks work like wires and connect the different parts of a circuit to each other.

Plastic Fantastic!

If it weren't for plastic, you'd have to work a lot harder at home. Smooth plastic surfaces are easy to clean with a wipe. Old wooden kitchen tables had to be scrubbed with disinfectant to keep them clean. Modern nonstick saucepans are easier to clean than old iron or enamel pans. In the bathroom, toothbrushes with plastic bristles are easier to clean than old brushes made of animal hair. Modern paints and varnishes contain plastic, giving them a durable, long-lasting, easy-to-clean surface. Without plastic, you'd have to repaint surfaces more often and spend much more time cleaning them. Plastic makes life much easier.

HOW WOULD YOU LIKE to brush your teeth with animal hair? It sounds disgusting, but before brushes were made of plastic, toothbrush bristles were made of stiff hair from a horse or boar.

IRON AND STEEL turn to rust if they get wet. They have to be polished or painted to protect them. Plastic doesn't rust, so it doesn't have to be polished or painted.

Iron and steel turn to rust because of a chemical reaction between the metal, water, and oxygen in the air. Plastic doesn't rust because it doesn't react chemically with water and oxygen.

Iron chain

Plastic chain

OUTDOORS in damp weather, wood can rot quickly unless protected with a coat of preservative, varnish, or paint. Now, there are doors and window frames made of plastic.

A STICKY PROBLEM. If there were no plastic sticky tape, you'd have to make do with tape made of paper or fabric. Paper tears and fabric tape is thick and ugly.

21

Make It From Plastic

About 280 million tons (250 million metric tons) of plastic is made every year. Newly made plastic looks like brightly colored gravel. To make things from it, it is heated until it melts. Chemicals may be added to make it harder, softer, or a different color. Gas may be blown into it to make foam plastic. The hot plastic is forced into a mold. The mold is cooled to harden the plastic. One molding machine can make hundreds or even thousands of identical plastic products a day. A variety of different manufacturing methods are used, including injection molding, extrusion, drawing, and blow molding.

DRAWING. Fibers are made by forcing hot plastic through tiny holes in a disc called a spinneret (right). Cold water hardens the fibers.

Plastic granules go in

EXTRUSION. Melted plastic is forced through a die (metal block) with a large hole in it. Plastic rods, bars, and pipes are made like this.

INJECTION MOLDING. Melted plastic is forced into a mold. Cold water cools the mold. It splits open and the perfectly formed plastic product falls out into a waiting bin.

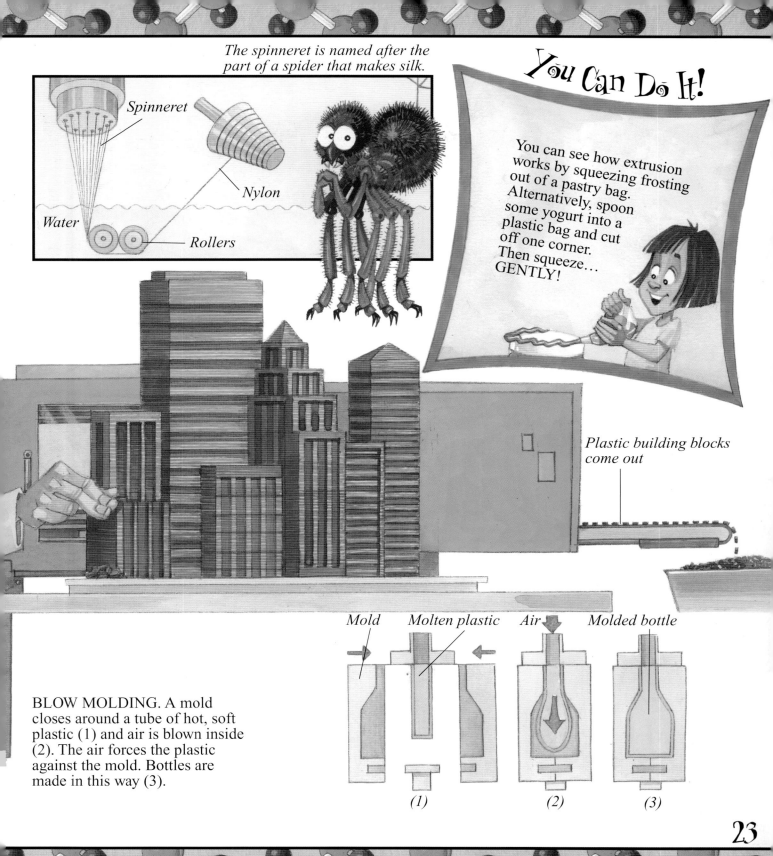

The spinneret is named after the part of a spider that makes silk.

Spinneret

Nylon

Water

Rollers

You Can Do It!

You can see how extrusion works by squeezing frosting out of a pastry bag. Alternatively, spoon some yogurt into a plastic bag and cut off one corner. Then squeeze… GENTLY!

Plastic building blocks come out

BLOW MOLDING. A mold closes around a tube of hot, soft plastic (1) and air is blown inside (2). The air forces the plastic against the mold. Bottles are made in this way (3).

Mold   Molten plastic   Air   Molded bottle

(1)   *(2)*   *(3)*

23

Carbon Fiber

1. MATS of woven carbon fiber are laid in a mold and soaked in resin (liquid plastic).

2. THE MOLD is sealed inside a plastic bag and the air is sucked out to squash the layers together.

3. THE MOLD, in the plastic bag, is heated in an oven called an autoclave to harden the plastic.

4. WHEN THE AUTOCLAVE has cooled down, the finished carbon fiber part can be taken out. The plastic resin has set, locking the carbon fiber mats together.

Super Strength

Some plastics are strong enough to stop a bullet. Some of them are fireproof, too. These plastics are used to make superstrong clothing to protect motorcyclists, firefighters, and auto-racing drivers. Ordinary plastics can be made stronger by combining them with another material. The new material is called a composite. Plastic composites are stronger than each of the materials they contain. Carbon fiber reinforced plastic, also known as carbon fiber, is a composite material ten times stronger and four times lighter than steel. Sports equipment such as tennis rackets, golf clubs, and ice hockey sticks are often made of carbon fiber. It's used to make race cars, too.

COMPOSITE MATERIALS are replacing metal parts in airliners. The Boeing 787 Dreamliner (below) has more composite parts than any other airliner. Half of its body and wings are made of composites.

Superstrong fireproof suit

Carbon fiber is such a strong material because of all the fibers inside it. When something tries to bend it, the plastic spreads the force across lots of fibers.

Carbon fiber car body

SMOOTH BOATS made of carbon fiber slip through the water easily and quickly. The worms, barnacles, and other sea life that often damage wooden boats can't get a grip on supersmooth plastic.

Plastic Problems

Plastic has great advantages, but it also has problems. In time, plastic parts and products break, wear out, or just become unfashionable and have to be replaced. Old unwanted wood, food, and natural fibers rot and eventually dissolve and disappear. Discarded plastic, however, can last for hundreds of years before it breaks down. One way to stop it piling up in landfills, and polluting the earth and water as it breaks down, is to use it again to make new things. This is called recycling. Another way is to burn it in a power station to make electricity.

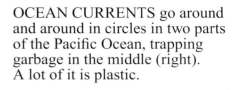

OCEAN CURRENTS go around and around in circles in two parts of the Pacific Ocean, trapping garbage in the middle (right). A lot of it is plastic.

Hmmm. That looks tasty!

ANIMALS might prefer a world without plastic. Countless turtles and seabirds have been killed by eating plastic in the sea, because they don't know it's bad for them.

LARGE plastic containers are reused as water carriers in developing countries. The lightweight plastic enables people to carry water over long distances a little more easily.

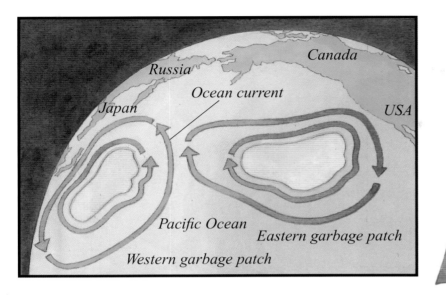

Russia

Canada

Japan

Ocean current

USA

Pacific Ocean

Eastern garbage patch

Western garbage patch

You Can Do It!

Look for triangular recycling marks on plastic bottles in your home. Make a note of the different plastics you find. Which is the most common?

DID YOU KNOW that you might be wearing recycled plastic? Plastic drink bottles are recycled to make the fibers that produce fleece jackets. It takes 25 plastic bottles to make one jacket.

PLASTIC BOTTLES can be recycled by being used to help build houses. The bottles are filled with sand or mud. Empty bottles can also be used to build greenhouses for growing plants.

DIFFERENT PLASTICS need to be recycled separately, so recyclers need to know which plastics they have. Some products have a triangle mark with a number to show the type of plastic. For example, 6 = PS = polystyrene. It's called the Resin Identification Code.

Resin Identification Codes

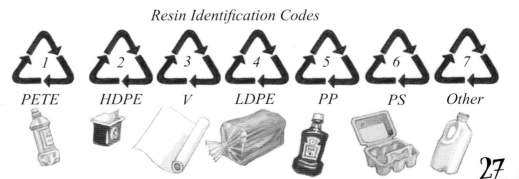

| 1 PETE | 2 HDPE | 3 V | 4 LDPE | 5 PP | 6 PS | 7 Other |

27

Looking Into the Future

Scientists are still creating new plastics and improving old ones. Most plastics are made from chemicals that come from oil, but oil causes pollution, and it will run out one day. Don't worry, you won't have to do without plastic. Future plastics will probably be made from natural materials, just as the first plastics were. They are called bioplastics. They're made from starch and cellulose produced by plants. Some bottles, packaging, and car parts already contain bioplastics. There are also new plastics that "heal" when they are cut. Products made from them will never show scratches. You'll wonder how we ever lived without plastic!

New Technologies

CLEVER PACKAGING. There are new plastics that change color when bacteria grow on them. Food packaging made of this plastic will tell you if the food inside is no longer safe to eat.

PRINT IT. Already people can make small plastic objects by using a 3D printer to print them. The printer makes things by building up one layer of plastic on top of another.

It's my new TV!

BENDY SCREENS. Nearly all screens on computers and other devices are made of hard, flat glass or plastic. Future plastic screens might be as thin and flexible as a sheet of paper.

Recycling plastic saves energy. It takes only about a quarter of the energy to make a plastic bottle from recycled plastic as it does to make the same bottle from new materials.

It's for making plastic!

PLASTIC MONEY. Australia, Canada, and New Zealand have changed from paper banknotes to plastic. More countries are likely to join them. Plastic banknotes last longer than paper.

Glossary

3D Three-dimensional: having length, width, and depth.

Atom The smallest particle of a chemical element.

Bacteria Microscopic living organisms. Many kinds of bacteria are harmless or useful to us, but some are dangerous because they cause diseases.

Blow molding A way of forming hollow plastic objects like bottles by closing a mold around a tube of hot, soft plastic, and blowing air inside.

Canopy A covering such as the see-through top of a fighter plane's cockpit.

Casein A substance found in milk.

Cellulose A substance found in plant fibers and the walls of plant cells.

Composite material A material made by combining two or more materials, such as carbon fiber reinforced plastic.

Disinfectant A cleaning product, usually liquid, that kills bacteria.

Drawing A way of forming fibers by forcing plastic, or another substance, through tiny holes in a block of metal.

Electronic circuit A pathway along which an electric current can flow, usually through a series of electronic devices that use the electrical energy to do work.

Extrusion A way of forming plastic rods, bars, and pipes by forcing hot, soft plastic through a block of metal with a large hole in it.

Factory A building or buildings where products are manufactured.

Fiber A thread of natural material (such as cotton) or synthetic material (such as nylon or rayon).

Gearwheel A toothed wheel. Also known as a gear or cog, usually found in small machines.

Injection molding A way of forming plastic by forcing hot liquid plastic into a mold and then cooling it.

Lifestyle A way of living for one person or a group of people.

Manufacture To make products for sale, usually in large numbers.

Microchip A small package of electronic parts forming one or more electronic circuits in one small block of plastic. Also called a chip, integrated circuit, or IC.

Molecule A group of atoms linked together.

Monomer A molecule that is linked to lots of other identical molecules to form a long, chain-like molecule called a polymer.

Oxygen One of the gases in air. Oxygen makes up about 20 percent (a fifth) of the air you breathe. Most of the rest is another gas called nitrogen.

Pollution Unwanted and sometimes harmful substances in the environment, especially in the air or water.

Polymer A long, chain-like molecule made of lots of identical units called monomers linked together.

Space age The period of history that began with the first spaceflight on October 4, 1957.

Starch A natural substance found in plants.

Superglue A very strong, quick-setting glue made of a plastic polymer called cyanoacrylate.

Synthetic Made artificially, by combining substances in a way that does not happen in nature.

Tinplate Thin sheets of iron or steel coated with a layer of tin.

Index

Top Inventors of Plastic

Alexander Parkes (1813–1890)
Parkes was born in Birmingham, England. He worked at a metal casting company that made things by pouring molten metal into molds. He dreamed up dozens of inventions, including new ways to process metal and strengthen it. Then, in 1841, he invented a way of using rubber to make fabric waterproof. Fifteen years later, he invented the plastic that was named after him, Parkesine.

Leo Baekeland (1863–1944)
Leo Henricus Arthur Baekeland was born in Ghent, Belgium. He studied chemistry and became a chemistry professor. In 1891, he moved to the United States, and two years later he invented a new type of photographic paper. In 1897, he became an American citizen. Then he experimented with chemicals to make new materials. In 1909, he announced his invention of Bakelite and set up a company to make Bakelite products. He retired in 1939 and died five years later at the age of 80.

Wallace Carothers (1896–1937)
Wallace Hume Carothers was born in Burlington, Iowa. He excelled in chemistry in college and went to work for the DuPont chemical company. There, he led a team of scientists who invented a synthetic rubber called Neoprene in 1930. Five years later he invented nylon.

Fire!

The first movies were photographed on film made from a plastic called celluloid. One of celluloid's disadvantages is that it catches fire very easily and burns quickly. When it burns, it produces poisonous smoke. Even if celluloid doesn't catch fire, it breaks down chemically over time. The clear film turns yellow, becomes sticky, and blisters. Eventually it falls apart altogether. The older it is, the more dangerous it becomes. It can even explode without warning! It's so dangerous that it can't even be thrown away. It has to be dealt with by experts. The oldest movies are kept in special fireproof storerooms until they can be copied onto modern film or recorded digitally.

A safer plastic film replaced celluloid in the 1940s. It was known as safety film. Although safety film doesn't burst into flames, it has another problem. After a few years, it begins to break down, giving off the telltale smell of vinegar. As the film breaks down it shrinks and becomes brittle. Colors on the film begin to fade, too. Films photographed on safety film can be rescued by copying them onto new film or recording them digitally.

Frank Miller

W9-CCW-296

Frank Miller

FABERGÉ

IMPERIAL EGGS
and other fantasies

for Charlotte
and her mother

FABERGÉ

IMPERIAL EGGS
and other fantasies

by
Hermione Waterfield
and
Christopher Forbes

Illustrated with works from
The FORBES Magazine Collection, New York

BRAMHALL HOUSE • NEW YORK

Copyright © 1978 by Forbes Inc.
All rights reserved. No part of this book may be
reproduced in any form without the permission of
Charles Scribner's Sons or Forbes Inc.

This edition is published by Bramhall House, a
division of Clarkson N. Potter, by arrangement with
Forbes Inc.

b c d e f g h

BRAMHALL HOUSE 1980 EDITION

Manufactured in the United States of America

Library of Congress Cataloging in Publication Data

Waterfield, Hermione.
  Fabergé imperial eggs and other fantasies.

  Bibliography: p. 14.
    1. Faberzhe, Karl Gustavovich, 1846-1920—Catalogs.
2. Faberzhe (Firm)—Catalogs.   3. Easter eggs—Russian
Republic—Catalogs.   4. Art objects, Russian—Catalogs.
5. Forbes magazine—Art collections—Catalogs.
I. Forbes, Christopher, joint author.   II. Faberzhe,
Karl Gustavovich, 1846-1920.   III. Faberzhe (Firm)
IV. Title.
NKNK7398.F32A4 1980   739.2'092'4   80-15935
ISBN: 0-517-32094-0

Color photography: H. Peter Curran
Black and white photography: Robert Forbes
Original illustrations: B. Robert Shapiro
Typography: Trentypo Inc.

CONTENTS

ACKNOWLEDGMENTS

To Margaret Kelly, who had to redo much of what we did to make this book readable.

To Dr. Everett Fahy of the Frick Collection, who deserves our gratitude for his kindness in writing the essay which appears after the Introduction to this catalogue. He offers an intriguing and enlightening historical perspective to Fabergé's ingenious objects.

To the Schaffer Family of A La Vieille Russie, without whose help over the years there would have been very little to catalogue in this book. Also for their kindness in allowing us access to some of the books in their collection.

To A. Kenneth Snowman, whose books, articles and memorable exhibitions have done so much to stimulate an appreciation of Fabergé, for his help and generous permission to reproduce a number of photographs.

To Jessie McNab of The Metropolitan Museum, who has so kindly shared her time and knowledge on the many occasions we have turned to her.

To Prince Leonid Lieven, whose unselfish assistance is much appreciated, and to John Mollo, who identified the uniforms which appear in a number of miniatures.

To Gwendolyn Kelso, who has shared so graciously the fruits of her research and her knowledge of gems and stones.

To the late Lansdell Christie's personal assistant, Miss Sternberg, for her help in documenting several of the pieces acquired from his estate.

To Marilyn Swezey, especially for her knowledge of Russian, which had made it possible for us to do research from which we otherwise would have been precluded.

To Peter Curran, whose color photographs help make this book so visually sumptuous, and to Robert Forbes, whose black and white photographs facilitate the presentation of details of certain objects otherwise difficult to describe.

To Buddy Shapiro, whose drawings make it possible to catalogue Fabergé's incredible Imperial Eggs without the distracting contrasts inherent in photographs taken over many years by many different photographers.

To Amanda Waterfield and Lisa Lorillard, without whose research the histories of the objects catalogued would have been less complete.

To JoAnne Samaniego, without whose typing skills the printer would never have been able to decipher the manuscript.

To Joe Ramos and Jimmy Callahan of the FORBES security staff, without whose watchful attention and careful handling it would have been impossible to examine and photograph so many works of art.

Lastly, and for those who enjoy this book, perhaps most importantly, to all those at Trentypo, Inc. and most especially Chet Zuczek, as well as to Albert A. Colacello and his colleagues at Princeton Polychrome, without whom the labors of all those listed previously would never have been brought together into this splendid new volume devoted to Fabergé.

Our sincerest thanks,

HERMIONE WATERFIELD
CHRISTOPHER FORBES

FOREWORD

The 300-year-old Romanov dynasty came to an abrupt end on July 16, 1918 when the Czar Nicholas II, his wife, and five children were murdered in the cellar of a Siberian house during one of the bloodiest wars of all time. Not too many months after the governmental chaos that followed, Russia became the modern world's first Communist state.

When very young I read with horrified fascination an abundantly illustrated volume on World War I. Its chapter about the Russian Revolution and the massacre of the Romanov family included a picture of a Fabergé Imperial Egg to illustrate the pre-War extravagance of Russia's rulers.

In London many years later (but longer ago than I like to remember), I bought my wife a Fabergé cigarette box (Catalogue no. 64) for Christmas. Since then she has treasured and constantly used it—until recently, when I 'borrowed' it to be part of our permanent Fabergé exhibition in the lobby of the FORBES Magazine Building.

Before we met and married, she, too, had been fascinated by Fabergé's fabulous combination of fantasy and artistry. The first acquisition was exciting for us both.

Our second personal Fabergé piece came a couple of years later when I presented her with a wee charm bracelet-sized egg of white enamel with an enameled red cross (Catalogue no. 30). This too has been 'borrowed' and is now also on display at FORBES.

Our first major acquisition was the Duchess of Marlborough Egg (Catalogue no. 9) from a Parke-Bernet auction. It cost us three-and-a-half times the gallery's estimate, and I was torn between the thrill of having it and a sinking feeling that perhaps we had overbid as a result of auction fever.

Reassurance was swift, though, when the late Alexander Schaffer, founder of Fifth Avenue's A La Vieille Russie, identified himself as the underbidder and invited me to view the major Fabergé masterpieces in his safe.

In time, when there was money to match desire, we added to the FORBES Magazine Collection the Fifteenth Anniversary Egg (Catalogue no. 6) presented by Czar Nicholas II to his wife on the 15th anniversary of their coronation, and the Orange Tree Egg (Catalogue no. 7).

The greatest addition at any one time came when the Christie Collection, on 'permanent' exhibition at the Metropolitan Museum of Art, came on the market soon after Mr. Christie's death. His widow asked Mr. Schaffer, who played a key part in building that collection, to handle its sale. Mr. Schaffer and I had come to know each other well during those many times I haunted his fabulous premises, as well as on the many occasions he had acted as agent and counsellor to FORBES in our frequently successful bidding at auctions in London and elsewhere.

As a result he gave me first crack at the Christie Collection. We bought not only the two Imperial Eggs, the Spring Flowers Egg (Catalogue no. 3) and the Chanticleer Egg (Catalogue no. 5), but a number of the most beautiful things we now have.

Fortunately, from the pocketbook point of view, I have never been too much turned on by Fabergé's animals nor, with a few exceptions, his flowers. There was only one animal in the extensive Christie Collection that I was anxious to have — the Polar Bear (Catalogue no. 60). The present Aga Khan bought all the others and, as a result, has one of the greatest Fabergé zoos in the world.

From time to time we are able to add little things and big things, but the time between times grows greater as Fabergé prices soar. Those who know most about these matters tell us that our collection is now worth many times what it cost. As the son of a canny Scotsman, I like to believe it so.

But I hope we never have to find out.

MALCOLM S. FORBES
New York, 1973

POSTSCRIPT

In the five years since my father wrote the foreword to the first book devoted to the FORBES Magazine Collection of Fabergé, reprinted above, the number of objects in the collection has almost doubled.

Certainly the most exciting of these recent acquisitions has been that of the three Imperial Eggs. The First Egg (Catalogue no. 1), while much simpler than those which followed, represents an interesting combination of fantasy and history. Ironically, the Egg which preceded the First into the collection, the Cross of St. George Egg (Catalogue no. 8), was the last presented. Fabergé himself delivered it to the Dowager Empress in 1916. It is also the only Imperial Egg to leave Russia in the possession of its original owner. The Resurrection Egg (Catalogue no. 2) is a technical *tour-de-force* which foreshadows the splendid genius of later, larger eggs.

Other Imperial pieces of much appeal are the Silver Paddle Steamer (Catalogue no. 50) which was presented to the Czarevitch in 1913, and later belonged to President Franklin Roosevelt; and the Heart Surprise Frame (Catalogue no. 71) made to commemorate the birth of Nicholas II's daughter Tatiana in 1897. A personal favorite and the last piece purchased as this book went to press is the ravishing Blue Rocaille Presentation Box (Catalogue no. 62) with its surprise miniature of the young Czar Nicholas II.

Not all Fabergé is Imperial or grand, but even the most modest objects are brilliantly executed. Fabergé's incredible sense of design and appropriateness of materials makes a pair of ruby-mounted, ebony-shafted knitting needles (Catalogue no. 92) seem very natural, until the intellectual absurdity of them makes the Russian Revolution appear inevitable.

History is not without its amusing ironies. In September, 1917, one month before the Soviets seized power in Russia, B.C. Forbes published the first issue of FORBES Magazine. Sixty-one years later, the "Capitalist Tool," as FORBES is known, owns only two fewer of Fabergé's Imperial Eggs than the Soviet Government.

CHRISTOPHER FORBES
New York, 1978

INTRODUCTION

The Czar ruled supreme over all Russia. Alexander III, after having seen his father assassinated as he stooped to help an injured coachman, determined his reign would be totally autocratic. He was next only to God. The Romanov Dynasty had been on the Russian throne for nearly three hundred years, expanding frontiers to include people of widely different cultures and tongues and inviting painters and craftsmen to decorate palaces. There seemed no reason why the Romanovs should not continue for many years ahead to rule their territories of "all the Russias." The Court gathered in the fine palaces of St. Petersburg about the beautiful Czarina Maria Feodorovna.

ORIGINS   Into this city Peter Carl Fabergé was born in 1846. His forbears were French Huguenots who were compelled to leave Picardy after the revocation of the Edict of Nantes, when Louis XIV deprived the Protestants in France of their religious and civil liberties in 1685. The first of the Fabergé family to become a Russian citizen was Carl's grandfather, Peter. He settled in Pernau in Estonia. It was here that Carl's father, Gustav, was born and later married Charlotte Jungstedt. In 1843, after his apprenticeship to a jeweller, Gustav Fabergé opened a shop in a basement of Bolshaya Morskaya Street in St. Petersburg.

YOUTH   He sent his eldest son, Peter Carl, to the Gymnasium Svetaya Anna and, when he retired to Dresden, to the Handelschule there. Whilst he was in Dresden the young Carl would have seen the wonders of the Grünes Gewölbe Museum including Dinglinger's superb "At the Court of the Grand Mogul," and the Egg Casket by Le Roy, his copy of which is now in the FORBES Collection (Catalogue no. 4). The young man was expected to become a jeweller like his father and was apprenticed to the goldsmith Friedmann in Frankfurt. He paid visits to Rome, Venice, Florence, London and Paris. While in these cities he may well have discussed methods and problems with jewellers, examined their techniques and watched the results of their experiments.

Carl Fabergé returned to St. Petersburg and in 1870 took control of his father's firm from the manager, Zaiontchovsky. His brother, Agathon, who had been undergoing the same apprenticeship on his own, joined him there in 1882. Here, then, were two young men, full of ideas and energy (though Agathon was to die in 1895). They exhibited at the Pan-Russian exhibition of 1882 and won a gold medal. The fantasies and small, hardstone animals that were among their exhibits must have been a refreshing change from the dazzle of diamonds and gold on neighboring stands, and drew a great deal of attention. Among those whom they attracted was the Czar himself. Alexander III saw the possibilities of these fantasies to relieve the gloom that often possessed his wife since the assassination of his father. His fascination with these early Fabergé creations ultimately culminated in the series of Imperial Easter Eggs.

WORK   The business grew. A branch was opened in Moscow in 1887, others in Odessa and Kiev in the south followed. In 1898, No. 24 Bolshaya Morskaya Street (the same street as his father's original shop) was purchased and a magnificent edifice was begun, eventually to contain apartments for Peter Carl and four floors of workshops as well as the shop on the ground floor. As Fabergé made nothing himself, he was dependent on his workshops to supply him with

pieces of the quality he demanded. But these workshops were autonomous units, the men being hired, paid and instructed by their workmasters. It was not rare for workmasters to produce pieces for more than one shop, but Fabergé saw the advantages of having his most important workmasters in the same building as the designers and himself. No time would be wasted putting on coats and hurrying through streets, and he was constantly available for advice and discussion. Thus he could combine difficult materials with the virtuosity which is his hallmark. In the new building, completed in 1900, Hollming was installed on the first floor, above him was the best-known of the goldsmiths, Perchin, succeeded on his death by Wigström. The jeweller Holmström was on the third, and above him another jeweller, Thielemann. The silverware was made at the old premises under the workmaster Rappoport.

Occasionally Fabergé's staff, which at one point numbered over 700 men at all the branches, could not keep up with the demands made by customers, and outsiders would be commissioned. Perhaps the best-known of these is Fedor Rückert who would usually be commissioned for silverware enamelled in the old Russian style with the muted colors so distinctive to Fabergé. The Moscow branch was the only shop to employ the workmen directly, so after the House of Fabergé was granted the Royal Warrant in 1884 they used the Imperial eagle above their punch "Fabergé." That the St. Petersburg workshops did not also use the eagle was explained by Andrea Marchetti to Kenneth Snowman. "You see, in Moscow it was the firm who made the piece and of course the firm, as a Royal Warrant holder, was entitled to the use of the Imperial Cipher; but in St. Petersburg you will notice that each piece is signed by the particular workmaster responsible for its manufacture, so really it was not the firm's production at all, but the original work of the man whose signature it bore—and that man, whether it was Perchin, Wigström, or any other, was not entitled to the Royal Cipher—and that is why you never find it on St. Petersburg pieces."

THE MAN   Peter Carl Fabergé presided over this empire with pride and care. In his book, H. C. Bainbridge tells us that he was a very sensitive man, of quiet demeanor and good humor but quick-tempered and sarcastic if provoked. His instruction to Bainbridge on the occasion of the latter's appointment to the firm was "Be noble." He favored well-cut tweed suits. He lived under great tension, for he never knew what crowned head or other important person would arrive unannounced to demand "something new." His designers and workmasters constantly consulted him. According to tradition, new pieces would be brought for his inspection and placed upon a sheet of metal on his desk. If a piece did not meet with his approval he smashed it with a hammer kept for this purpose. Many feel he should have smashed more pieces, but they misread his motives. The pieces would be smashed if some fault appeared in the workmanship, not in the taste. Fabergé had to cater to a widely differing public with a variety of tastes, so he produced both the sugary confection of the Duchess of Marlborough Egg (Catalogue no. 9), and the strikingly modern lines of the Kovsh (Catalogue no. 135). Besides the Russian Imperial Family and aristocracy, among his most admiring and august clients were King Edward VII of England and King Rama of Siam. The latter was introduced to the works of Fabergé by Prince Chakrebong who had married a Russian and was a Colonel in the Regiment of Hussars. Fabergé was invited to meet both Kings, but apparently never did — in fact he fled London when he learned he would be expected to seek audience with Queen Alexandra.

No, it was workmanship that was all-important. In this way he resembled the European goldsmiths of previous centuries and the Chinese, for it was not the value of the materials that mattered to him but rather what had been wrought from them. He derived a sense of achievement by enlarging boundaries of technical skill and combining new materials successfully to produce greater varieties. His contemporaries admired him. When his son, Alexander, was sent to Paris to learn how to improve the techniques of enamelling from the celebrated Houillon, the latter was astonished and remarked, "We in Paris are quite unable to do the things you appear to do so easily in St. Petersburg." Many of his contemporaries produced pieces similar to those from the firm of Fabergé, and for simple cigarette cases, buckles, clocks and such, they could produce as fine. But no one made a more precise collet for a stone, or conceived the balance of metal and color for a fantasy piece better than Fabergé. The simplicity of the Orange Tree Egg (Catalogue no. 7) belies the exquisite workmanship necessary to produce it.

IMITATORS Like all successful people, he had imitators who produced work purporting to be from his workshops, and the revolution lent confusion to aid them. Here we are confronted with the problem of how to tell a genuine piece of Fabergé from one of his competitors or imitators. There is no short cut. The marks can be a guide but the eye is a better one, and the most reliable judge is an informed eye. Even then, informed experts can differ over a few objects. To add further confusion, spurious marks have been applied not only to manifest imitations of Fabergé, but also as embellishments to genuine pieces and on old Russian pieces from other houses.

Christie's sold a silver snuff box hallmarked 1846 and stamped "Fabergé" — the year of his birth! Hardstone animals, figures and flowers have been and continue to be made in France and Germany as well as Italy and Switzerland and Russia.

THE END After the outbreak of hostilities with Germany, part of his shop was taken over for the manufacture of small arms and munitions. In any case, many of his clients were now fighting at the front, their families engaged in activities such as the Red Cross, in which the Imperial Family was so involved, and communications with clients abroad was difficult, to say the least. However, he continued to produce the Imperial Easter Eggs and as many other fantasies as possible under the circumstances. After the abdication of Nicholas II and his subsequent arrest by the Provisional Government, the situation worsened, until finally the Bolsheviks seized power and Fabergé was forced to flee the country. He left, posing as a courier to the British Embassy, in September, 1918, and arrived in Wiesbaden via Riga, Berlin, Frankfurt and Hamburg. Meanwhile, his wife had fled to Sweden with their son Eugéne. They eventually met again in Lausanne in 1920. Another son, Agathon, stayed in Russia until after 1923.

When the Bolsheviks seized the shop they continued to operate it on a reduced basis. The late Alexander Schaffer would tell how the Soviets would "finish" an uncompleted piece or try to twin things up in order to sell them. Finally all the workmen left and the stock was sold or removed. The premises are still used as a shop, but of an inferior, nondescript variety.

Fabergé died on September 24, 1920, and after his wife's death in Cannes on January 27, 1925, Eugène brought his father's ashes to be buried with his mother's beneath a tombstone of Swedish black porphyry inscribed "CHARLES FABERGE, joaillier de la Cour de Russie, né 18 mai 1846 à St. Petersburg, décédé 24 septembre 1920 à Lausanne. AUGUSTA FABERGE, née Jacobs née 25 décembre 1851 (vieux style à Tsarskoe Selo, décédé 27 janvier 1925 (nouveau style) à Cannes." Two of his sons, Eugène and Alexander, together with Andrea Marchetti and a former rival, Giulio Guerrieri, set up a business in Paris as jewellers, goldsmiths and agents of their father's work. The shop was closed after Eugène's death in 1960 (Alexander predeceased him in 1952), but their resources were very limited. The story of Fabergé really ends in that autumn of 1918, when the head of the great firm left his emporium and history closed the doors behind the last of the great mastercraftsmen. A tradition of centuries was ended, yet to be revived.

HERMIONE WATERFIELD

FABERGÉ
PART OF A EUROPEAN TRADITION

To most of us today the name Peter Carl Fabergé conjures up memories of the extravagance and whimsicality enjoyed by a doomed society. It is impossible to think of him without recalling the surprise Easter Eggs and bejeweled mechanical trifles that he made to amuse the last of the Romanovs. We look at his work with mingled emotions. Inevitably, one yields to the fascination of gold and precious stones, and one is caught by the spell of his intricate craftsmanship. Yet for many of us there is an added interest, the tragic fate suffered by the Romanovs. Their costly indulgences symbolize, at least in part, one of the causes of their downfall.

Although Fabergé's works may strike some eyes as highly capricious, they belong to a well-established tradition of European goldsmith work—going back at least four centuries. His fanciful combinations of priceless jewels, enamelling, and beaten gold find parallels, for example, in the famous Rospiglioso Cup in the Metropolitan Museum of Art or in Benvenuto Cellini's salt-cellar, made for François I of France and now in the Kunsthistorisches Museum, Vienna. Like other monarchs, François I took special delight in highly ornamental decorative works. He also had a taste for the bizarre.

According to Giorgio Vasari, "When Leonardo was at Milan the King of France (François I) came there and desired him to do something curious; accordingly he made a lion whose chest opened after he had walked a few steps, discovering himself to be full of lilies." It is not known if Leonardo's lion was made of gold, but the idea of a mechanical contraption concealing a surprise brings many of Fabergé's creations to mind.

Fabergé's link with the Renaissance is not fortuitous. He actually made copies after the work of Renaissance goldsmiths in order to impress his patrons with his abilities. In the FORBES Magazine Collection the egg presented in 1894 by Alexander III to Maria Feodorovna (Catalogue no. 4) is modelled painstakingly after an egg-shaped casket now in the Grünes Gewölbe Museum at Dresden. The casket was made in the late seventeenth century by Le Roy, a goldsmith working in Amsterdam. Differing from the original only in minor details, Fabergé's copy is a *tour de force* and it is constructed, of course, to contain a mechanical surprise which unfortunately no longer survives.

The art of Fabergé is also deeply indebted to the great eighteenth-century French goldsmiths, who produced snuff boxes and other *objets d'art* for Louis XVI and the aristocratic society surrounding him. Again, in the FORBES Magazine Collection there is a striking example of Fabergé's skill in reproducing the style of a bygone epoch. A gold snuff box (Catalogue no. 66) is based directly upon a French box, which was housed in the Winter Palace in Fabergé's time and now also is in the FORBES Magazine Collection (Catalogue no. 65). Even his miniature sets of furniture, made from gold and semiprecious stones, are reproductions of earlier styles. The charming sedan chair in the FORBES Magazine Collection (Catalogue no. 49) takes us back to the eighteenth century in Venice. Nostalgia for the past is a characteristic running throughout Fabergé's work.

Fabergé's involvement with the past sets him apart from his contemporaries in Western Europe and America. Even in his time his works were not in any sense modern. To name the most prominent practitioners of the goldsmith's art during his lifetime underscores his individuality. The Americans, Charles Lewis Tiffany (1812-1902), and his son, Louis Comfort Tiffany (1848-1933), for instance, or the Frenchmen, Lucien Falize (1838-1897) and René Lalique (1860-1945) produced works in the Art Nouveau style. Charles Robert Ashbee (1863-1942), on the other hand, was one of the leaders of the Arts and Crafts movement in England. Georg Jensen (1866-1935), a Danish gold and silversmith, and Joseph Maria Olbrich (1867-1908), a German architect who designed metalwork in the Jugendstil, likewise achieved international recognition for their modern styles. Working in Russia for an autocratic society, Peter Carl Fabergé created examples of the goldsmith's art that looked back to the past and by association connected the Czar with his European predecessors.

Of all the eggs in the FORBES Magazine Collection, the most intriguing is the Orange Tree Egg (Catalogue no. 7). It is naturalistically modelled with dark-green nephrite foliage. When the surprise button is pressed, the leaves open and a bird rises from the leaves, sings, and then automatically disappears.

It brings to mind a passage from W.B. Yeats' *Sailing to Byzantium*:

> But such a form as Grecian goldsmiths make
> Of hammered gold and gold enamelling
> To keep a drowsy Emperor awake
> Or set upon a golden bough to sing
> To lords and ladies of Byzantium
> Of what is past, or passing, or to come.

Yeats added a note to his poem, saying that "I have read somewhere that in the Emperor's palace at Byzantium was a tree made of gold and silver, and artifical birds that sang." One might add that just such a tree with a singing bird was made in 1911 for Nicholas II of Russia.

EVERETT FAHY

Dr. Fahy is the Director of The Frick Collection, New York.

BIBLIOGRAPHICAL ABBREVIATIONS

BOOKS

Bainbridge 1949
Henry Charles Bainbridge, *Peter Carl Fabergé, Goldsmith and Jeweller to the Russian Imperial Court: His Life and Work*, London, 1949. *An anecdotal history by the man who worked for Fabergé in London.*

Bainbridge 1966
Henry Charles Bainbridge, *Peter Carl Fabergé, Goldsmith and Jeweller to the Russian Imperial Court: His Life and Work*, London, 1966. *Same as 1949 edition except for rearrangement of plates, deletion of acknowledgments and addition of color dust jacket.*

Snowman 1953
A. Kenneth Snowman, *The Art of Carl Fabergé*, London, 1953. *Pioneering research book which contains more basic information on the House of Fabergé than any other. Many color plates.*

Snowman 1962
A. Kenneth Snowman, *The Art of Carl Fabergé*, 2nd ed. London, 1962. *1953 text revised. Many additional illustrations in color and black and white.*

Snowman 1964
A. Kenneth Snowman, *The Art of Carl Fabergé*, 3rd ed. London, 1964. *Same as 1962 except for addition and changes of a few plates.*

ARTICLES

Du/von Hapsburg
Geza von Hapsburg, "Carl Fabergé: Die glanzvolle Welt eines königlichen Juweliers," *Du*, December 1977, pp. 48-88. *Excellent plates, many in color. Good section on materials.*

Esquire
"Breakfast at Fabergé's," *Esquire*, November 1972, pp. 138-39. *Selected objects from the FORBES Magazine Collection.*

FORBES
"Carl Fabergé Knew His Business," *FORBES*, March 1, 1967-October 16, 1978. *A series of ads featuring color illustrations of pieces from the FORBES Magazine Collection. See Appendix C for a complete list.*

Great Private Collections/Snowman
A. Kenneth Snowman, "Lansdell K. Christie, New York: Objets d'art by Fabergé," in *Great Private Collections*, ed. Douglas Cooper, New York, 1963, pp. 240-49.

Home News/Cook
Winifred I. Cook, "Imperial Eggs by Fabergé," *The Home News*, April 10, 1977, pp. C1-C2. *Interview with M.S. Forbes about Fabergé; several black and white plates.*

Metropolitan Bulletin/McNab Dennis
Jessie McNab Dennis, "Fabergé's Objects of Fantasy," *The Metropolitan Museum of Art Bulletin*, March 1965, pp. 229-42. *A well illustrated discussion of pieces from the Lansdell K. Christie collection.*

Newseek/Douglas
Douglas Davis, "All that Glitters," *Newsweek*, June 11, 1973, pp. 82-83, 85. *Review of the exhibition of the FORBES Magazine Collection at the New York Cultural Center. Page of color illustrations.*

New Yorker
"Carl Fabergé Knew His Business," *The New Yorker*, February 11-August 12, 1967. *See FORBES.*

N.Y. Times/Reif
Rita Reif, "Fabergé in New York," *The New York Times*, September 2, 1977, p. C17. *Fabergé at FORBES and A La Vieille Russie. Syndicated.*

Nineteenth Century/Snowman
A. Kenneth Snowman, "Carl Fabergé in London," *Nineteenth Century*, Summer 1977, pp. 50-55. *Discussion of the Jubilee exhibition at the Victoria and Albert Museum.*

Palm Beach Life/Watts
William H. Watts, "Peter Carl Fabergé: Jeweler to the Czars," *Palm Beach Life*, March 1978, pp. 36-39. *Summary text, many color illustrations.*

Villager/Sears
David Sears, "Those Fabulous Eggs at Forbes," *The Villager*, August 8, 1974, pp. 3-5.

Vogue Italia/Clay
Roland Clay, "Fabergé: l'orafo degli Zar," *Vogue Italia*, November 1977, pp. 128-31. *Selected works from the FORBES Magazine Collection. All illustrated in color.*

EXHIBITIONS & CATALOGUES

ALVR 1961
"The Art of Peter Carl Fabergé," A La Vieille Russie, New York, October 25-November 7, 1961. *Catalogue includes 295 pieces with 112 black and white illustrations and 6 color illustrations.*

ALVR 1968
"The Art of the Goldsmith and the Jeweler," A La Vieille Russie, New York, November 6-23, 1968. *Catalogue includes 81 pieces of Fabergé, 72 of which are illustrated in black and white, 9 in color.*

Corcoran 1961
"Easter Eggs and Other Precious Objects by Carl Fabergé," The Corcoran Gallery of Art, Washington, D.C., 1961. *Catalogue of 110 pieces from the Lansdell K. Christie collection, including 26 color plates. See Collections Past, Appendix B.*

NYCC/Waterfield 1973
Hermione Waterfield, "Fabergé from the Forbes Magazine Collection," The New York Cultural Center, New York, April 11-May 22, 1973. *Catalogue of 82 pieces with 15 black and white illustrations and 32 color illustrations.*

V & A/Snowman 1977
A. Kenneth Snowman, "Fabergé: 1846-1920," Victoria and Albert Museum, London, June 23-September 25, 1977. *Catalogue of over 500 pieces including nearly 300 objects from the Royal Collection. There are 102 black and white illustrations and 48 color ones. Organized by case and collection, the catalogue lacks an index which hampers its usefulness. Particularly good plates of objects in the Royal Collection.*

NOTES

The maximum dimension of each object is given in inches followed by millimeters. Any supplementary dimensions are given in the same manner.

In those instances where objects are not reproduced close to actual size, the percentage of reduction is indicated in parentheses.

All marks are given in Roman characters. Cyrillic equivalents where applicable, as well as the meaning of other marks and inscriptions, are listed below. In entries where no marks are included, it may be presumed that there are none.

Full references for books, catalogues, exhibitions and articles cited in more than six entries are included in the list of abbreviations on page 14.

MARKS

Workmasters (Appendix B for biographies and lists of works illustrated).

BA	Johan Victor AARNE
FA/ФA	Fedor AFANASSIEV
JA/ЯA	Karl Gustav Hjalmar ARMFELT
A*H	August Fredrik HOLLMING
AH	August Wilhelm HOLMSTRÖM
HH	Unidentified Fabergé workmaster
EK	Erik August KOLLIN
EK/ЭК	Unidentified Ovchinnikov workmaster (p. 104)
GL/ГЛ	G. LUNDELL
AN	Anders Johan NEVALAINEN
GN	Gabriel NIUKKANEN
MP/МП	Michael PERCHIN
OP	Knut Oskar PIHL
WR	Wilhelm REIMAR
FR/ФР	Fedor RÜCKERT
AT/◈	Alexander TILLANDER
AT	Alfred THIELEMANN
HW	Henrik WIGSTRÖM

Hall Inspectors

AP	Unidentified assayer
IL/ИЛ	I.S. LEBDKIN, Moscow after 1896
JL/ЯЛ	Jacob LYAPUNOV, St. Petersburg 1896-1903

City and Date of Manufacture

Alpha/α	St. Petersburg, 1908-17.
Anchors/⚓	St. Petersburg, through 1896, possibly later.
Delta/▲	Moscow, 1908-17.
St. George/🜨	Moscow, through 1896, possibly later.
Kokoshnik/🜨	All cities after c. 1896.

Other Marks

Crest—By appointment to the British Sovereign.
Eagle—Russian Imperial Warrant.
ET—French Import mark.
Swan—French Import mark used after 1893.

Metal Grades

56, 72	Gold content in "zolotniks," equivalent to 14, 18 karat gold.
84, 91	Silver content in "zolotniks," 91 being just above sterling.

Scratched Numbers

Many pieces have four or five digit numbers scratched unobtrusively on them. It is thought that these could be Fabergé inventory numbers. These and other later dealers' scratches are presented in the hope that if a Fabergé stock book ever comes to light, they may be of assistance.

EGGS

Easter is the most important festival of the Russian Orthodox Church. With the rebirth of Christ and the new hope of life spiritual comes spring and new hope of life physical. What better symbol of this rebirth than an egg? An egg is also something everyone can afford. Traditionally in Russia, as well as numerous other countries, eggs, dyed a variety of hues, are exchanged as gifts on Easter Sunday. Among those who can afford them there is an exchange of more elaborate gifts. Surely, however, none has ever equalled the ingenious and exotic fantasy of the eggs devised by Peter Carl Fabergé.

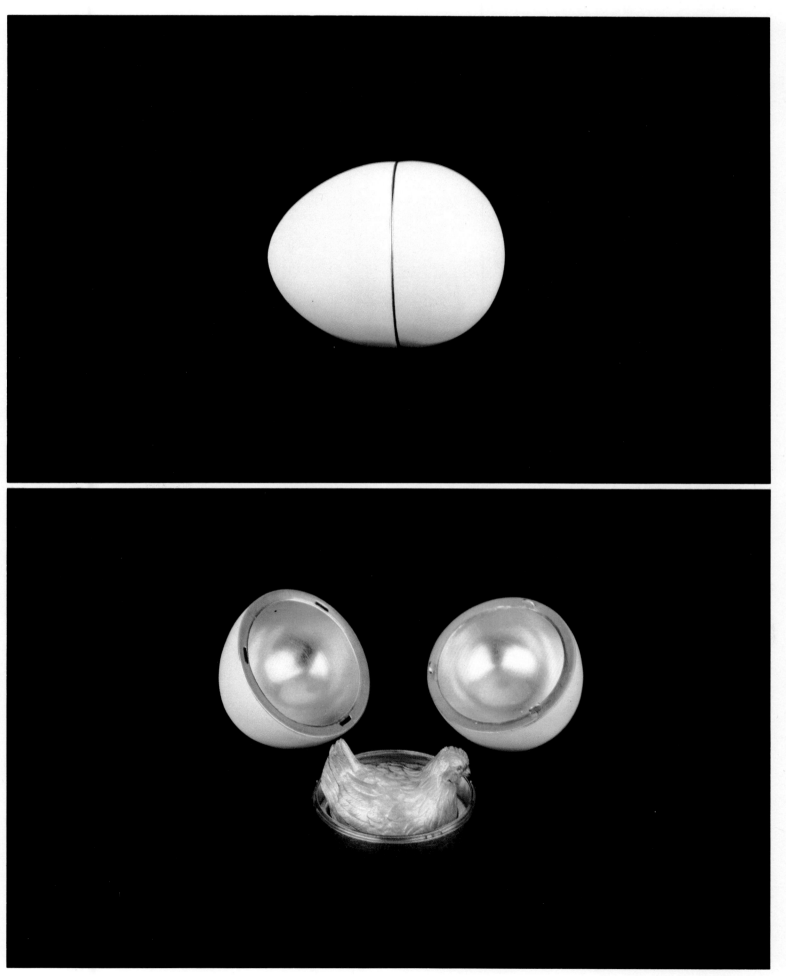

17

1. First Imperial Egg, open & closed

1. FIRST IMPERIAL EGG

2-1/2 in./64 mm.
YOLK: 1-9/16 in./40 mm.
HEN: 1-3/8 in./35 mm.
ACC. NO. FAB78001

The gold shell of this simple but historic piece is enamelled opaque white and polished to resemble a hen's egg. The two halves, joined by a bayonet fitting, open to reveal a matt gold yolk containing a nest of chased yellow-gold straw in which sits a naturalistically chased vari-colored-gold hen set with ruby eyes. In the tail feathers is a hinge on which the hen opens horizontally when the beak is lifted. Originally contained within was a diamond replica of the Imperial Crown which concealed a tiny ruby pendant suspended within it. The present whereabouts of these two tiny surprises is unknown.

As was often to be the case with later eggs, the idea for, if not the execution of, this egg was not original to Fabergé. Several examples by eighteenth-century goldsmiths and jewellers of eggs concealing hens containing surprises are known today. One such piece, recorded in the Danish Royal Collection as early as 1743, might well have been known to the Czarina, formerly Princess Dagmar of Denmark, and for this reason may have been selected by Fabergé to serve as a model for the First Imperial Egg.

PROVENANCE
Presented by Czar Alexander III to his wife, Maria Feodorovna, c.1886.
Anon. Sale: Christie's, London, March 15, 1934, Lot 55, catalogue p. 10 and preface. £85.
Lady Grantchester, wife of Sir Alfred Suenson-Taylor who was created 1st Baron Grantchester June 30, 1953.
A La Vieille Russie, New York.

EXHIBITIONS
"Special Coronation Exhibition of the Work of Carl Fabergé," Wartski, London, May 20-June 13, 1953, no. 156, catalogue p. 15.
V & A/Snowman 1977, no. O3, catalogue p. 94 reproduced.

REFERENCES
H. C. Bainbridge, *Twice Seven*, London, 1933, p. 174.
H. C. Bainbridge, "Preface—A Unique Collection of Objets d'Art Designed by Carl Fabergé," Christie's, London, March 15, 1934, unpaginated catalogue.
Geoffrey Harmsworth, "Easter Egg that Cost £5000," *The Daily Mail*, March 16, 1934, reproduced.
H. C. Bainbridge, "Russian Imperial Easter Gifts, The Work of Carl Fabergé," *The Connoisseur*, May 1934, p. 305.
H. J. Mayo, "Objects d'Art by Carl Fabergé," *The Connoisseur*, June 1934, p. 418.
Bainbridge 1949/66, p. 70.
Snowman 1953, pp. 72, 74, reproduced four times no. 280-283.
Parker Lesley, *Handbook of the Lillian Thomas Pratt Collection*, Virginia, 1960, p. 30.
Snowman 1962/64, pp. 76, 78, reproduced four times no. 313-316.
Great Private Collections/Snowman, p. 243.
"Fabulous Fabergé," *MD*, April 1967, pp. 270, 275, reproduced.

Donald Wintersgill, "Russian Fantasia," *Guardian Weekly*, November 1, 1969, p. 17.
Timothy Green, *The World of Gold*, New York, 1970, p. 32.
Howard Ricketts, *Antique Gold and Enamelware in Color*, New York, 1971, p. 109.
Henry H. Hawley, *Fabergé and His Contemporaries*, Cleveland, 1973, pp. 8, 72.
NYCC/Waterfield 1973, p. 12.
Betty Jo Shirley, "The Great Easter Egg Hunt," *Coast*, April 7, 1974, p. 82.
Parker Lesley, *Fabergé*, a Catalogue of the Lillian Thomas Pratt Collection of Russian Imperial Jewels, Virginia, 1976, p. 38.
Christine Masson and Claude Temple, "Le Monde Féerique de Fabergé," *L'Estampille*, February 15, 1976, p. 11.
Du/von Hapsburg, pp. 56, 62, 72.
Palm Beach Life/Watts, pp. 82-83.
Jean Nichols, "The Arts . . . and You," *News-Virginian*, Waynesboro, April 19, 1978.
Rita Reif, "Glittering Baubles Made For a Czar," *New York Times*, April 23, 1978, p. 23 (syndicated).

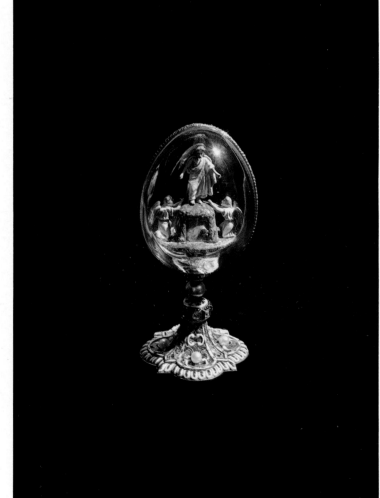

2. Resurrection Egg (reduced 27%)

2. RESURRECTION EGG

3-7/8 in./98 mm. high.
MARKS: *FABERGÉ*, 56 anchors, *MP* on rim; *56 anchors, MP* on base. (Perchin).
ACC. NO. FAB78002

Traditionally thought to have been the second Fabergé egg presented by Alexander III to his wife, this small but elaborate piece is a *tour de force* of the goldsmith's art. The carved rock crystal egg, the two halves of which are joined by a gold band set with diamonds, is supported on a gold quatrefoil base elaborately enamelled in the Renaissance style. Set amid the arabesques of translucent red, green, opaque white, blue and black enamel decorating the base are numerous tiny rose diamonds, four natural pearls, and eight brilliant diamonds in black enamelled collets. The shaft joining the base and the egg is comprised of a large natural pearl surmounted with a band of rose diamonds. Contained within the crystal shell is an exquisitely wrought group of Christ rising from the tomb flanked by two angels naturalistically enamelled *en ronde bosse*.

Only once again, three decades later, did Fabergé refer so directly to the religious significance of Easter —using a rendering of the Resurrection itself as the surprise for an Imperial Egg. In the Red Cross Egg of 1915, now in the Cleveland Museum, the Resurrection is treated two-dimensionally in the form of an icon rather than sculpturally as is the case with the earlier egg.

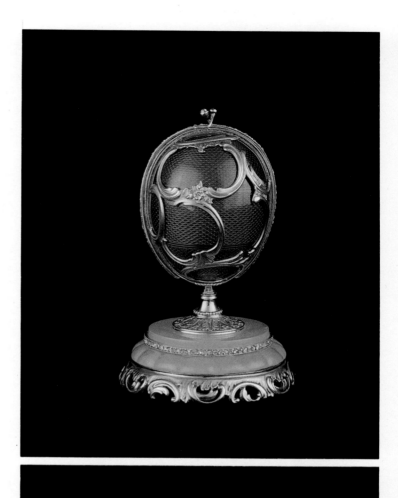

PROVENANCE
Presented by Czar Alexander III to his wife, Maria Feodorovna, c.1887.
Anon. Sale: Christie's, London, March 15, 1934, Lot 86, catalogue p. 16, reproduced on frontispiece. £110.
Lady Grantchester, wife of Sir Alfred Suenson-Taylor who was created 1st Baron Grantchester, June 30, 1953.
A La Vieille Russie, New York.

EXHIBITIONS
"Special Coronation Exhibition of the Work of Carl Fabergé," Wartski, London, May 20-June, 1953, no. 157, catalogue p. 16.
V & A/Snowman 1977, no. O4, catalogue p. 94, reproduced p. 95.

REFERENCES
Geoffrey Harmsworth, "Easter Egg that Cost £5000," *The Daily Mail*, March 16, 1934.
H. J. Mayo, "Objets d'Art by Carl Fabergé," *The Connoisseur*, June 1934, p. 418.
Snowman 1953, p. 75, reproduced no. 284.
Snowman 1962/64, p. 79, reproduced no. 317.
Du/von Hapsburg, p. 79.
Rita Reif, "Glittering Baubles Made for a Czar," *New York Times*, April 23, 1978, p. D24.

3. SPRING FLOWERS EGG

3-1/4 in./83 mm.
Basket: 1-1/2 in./33 mm.
MARKS: *MP, 56* inside left shell; *MP, 56* inside right shell; *MP, 56 anchors, FABERGÉ* on scroll work; scratched *44374*. (Perchin).
CASE: Original fitted velvet-covered egg shape; 5-3/8 in./138 mm.; liner stamped in gold *Eagle/FABERGÉ/St. Petersburg/Moscow London*.
ACC. NO. FAB66004

The small egg is enamelled a rich translucent strawberry on an engraved gold ground and applied with an elaborate chased green-gold rococo-style cagework. The ensemble is bisected by a band of red-gold set with rose diamonds surmounted by similarly set fasteners. When these are opened, the eggshell parts to reveal a miniature basket of wood anemones resting on a circular gold plinth. The platinum basket of open Gothic design is set with rose diamonds, and the flowers rising from translucent green enamelled engraved gold stems and leaves are comprised of six chalcedony petals and demantoid-set centers.

The egg rises from a short gold shaft emerging from a circular, rose diamond-girdled, carved bowenite base mounted on a band of chased gold scrollwork.

A similar basket of flowers was used for the surprise of the Winter Egg given by Nicholas II to his mother, Maria Feodorovna, in 1913.

PROVENANCE
Presented by Czar Alexander III to his wife, Maria
    Feodorovna, c. 1889.
Lansdell K. Christie, Long Island.
EXHIBITIONS
ALVR 1961, no. 290, p. 90, reproduced p. 89.
Corcoran 1961, no. 1, catalogue p. 24, reproduced in color
    p. 25 and on dust jacket.
Metropolitan 1962-66, no.L.62.8.1.
"In the Presence of Kings," The Metropolitan Museum of
    Art, New York, June-September 1967, no.L.67.31.1.
NYCC/Waterfield 1973, no. 1, catalogue pp. 4, 26, repro-
    duced in color p. 27.
V & A/Snowman 1977, no. L8, catalogue p. 73.
REFERENCES
Jeanne Horn, Hidden Treasure, How and Where to Find It,
    New York, 1962, Plate I, reproduced in color and on
    dust cover.
Snowman 1962/64, p. 81, reproduced in color Plate LXIX.
Great Private Collections/Snowman, p. 241 reproduced in
    color.
Metropolitan Bulletin/McNab Dennis, p. 240, reproduced
    no. 22.
"Fabulous Fabergé," MD, April 1967, p. 269, reproduced.
New Yorker, April 29, 1967, p. 117, reproduced in color.
FORBES, May 15, 1967, p. 62, reproduced in color.
Louise Bruner, "Fabulous Fabergé Easter Eggs," The Blade
    Sunday Magazine, April 14, 1968, p. 10, reproduced in
    color.
Donald Wintersgill, "Russian Fantasia," Guardian Weekly,
    November 1, 1969, p. 17.
Rosemary Disney, The Spendid Art of Decorating Eggs, New
    York, 1972, Plate XIX, reproduced in color.
FORBES, March 14, 1973, p. 96, reproduced in color.
Robert Cartmell, "Solid Gold Easter Eggs Fit For a Czar,"
    Times Union, Albany, April 26, 1973.
"Fabergé Show," The Village Voice, May 3, 1973, p. 46.
Newsweek/Douglas, p. 85, reproduced in color, p. 84.
Villager/Sears, p. 3.
V & A Coming Events, London, May-June 1977, reproduced
    in color.
N.Y. Times/Reif, p. C17.
Palm Beach Life/Watts, p. 37, reproduced in color.

4. RENAISSANCE EGG

5-1/4 in./140 mm.
MARKS: FABERGÉ, MP, 56 anchors inside base rim.
    (Perchin).
CASE: Original fitted velvet-covered egg shape; 8 in./203
    mm; lid lining stamp in gold obscured.
ACC. NO. FAB66001

This casket in the Renaissance style is the last of the eggs made for Czar Alexander III who died less than eight months after its presentation.

The egg is of translucent milky agate opening in half lengthwise, and all the mounts are of gold. The foot is enamelled with green leaves and red husks on a white ground. The upper half is covered by a white enamelled trellis set with four rose diamonds about a cabochon ruby at each intersection. At the center of the cover is the date 1894 in rose diamonds with enamelled devices set with rose diamonds and cabochon rubies; below a red enamelled border are similarly enamelled foliate devices set at intervals with diamonds; the lions' masks at either end have swing handles. This is almost identical to the gold and jeweled egg casket by Le Roy in the Grünes Gewölbe Museum, Dresden, Germany.

(Appendix D for Le Roy casket).

PROVENANCE
Presented by Czar Alexander III to his wife, Maria
    Feodorovna, 1894.
Hammer Galleries, New York.
H. T. de Vere Clifton.
Mr. and Mrs. Jack Linsky, New York.
A La Vieille Russie, New York.
EXHIBITIONS
Presentation of Imperial Russian Easter Gifts by Carl
    Fabergé, Hammer Galleries, New York, 1939, repro-
    duced in catalogue.
"Peter Carl Fabergé, Goldsmith and Jeweller to the
    Russian Imperial Court," A La Vieille Russie, New York,
    November-December, 1949, no. 123, catalogue p. 14.
"Loan Exhibition of the Art of Peter Carl Fabergé,"
    Hammer Galleries, New York, March 28-April 28,
    1951, p. 26, reproduced p. 23.
ALVR 1961, no. 292, catalogue pp. 16, 92, reproduced in
    color p. 90.
"Fabergé, Goldsmith to the Russian Imperial Court," M.
    H. de Young Memorial Museum, San Francisco, 1964,
    no. 148, pp. 38, 60, reproduced p. 60.
NYCC/Waterfield 1973, no. 2, catalogue pp. 6, 10, 28,
    reproduced in color, p. 29.
V & A/Snowman 1977, no. L15, catalogue, p. 74, reproduced
    in color p. 81.
REFERENCES
H. C. Bainbridge, Twice Seven, New York, 1937, repro-
    duced.
Bainbridge 1949/66, Plate 63(4), reproduced.
Snowman 1953, p. 78 reproduced twice nos. 291, 292.
Jeanne Horn, Hidden Treasure, How and Where to Find It,
    New York, 1962, Plate II, reproduced in color.
Henry Moscow, Russia under the Czars, New York, 1962,
    reproduced in color, p. 135.

4. *Renaissance Egg*

Snowman 1962-64, p. 84, reproduced in color Plate LXXII.

New Yorker, February 11, 1967, p. 15, reproduced in color.

FORBES, March 1, 1967, p. 44, reproduced in color.

"Fabulous Fabergé," *MD*, April 1967, p. 273, reproduced.

Edwin Fenton and John M. Good, *The Shaping of Western Society*, New York, p. 322, reproduced.

Rosemary Disney, *The Splendid Art of Decorating Eggs*, New York, 1972, Plate XVIII, reproduced in color.

Helen Harris, "The Russian Antique—An Exercise in Rarity," *Town & Country*, May 1976, p. 165.

Home News/Cook, reproduced twice pp. A1, C2.

"Build yourself a beautiful nest-egg at the East New York Savings Bank," (outdoor TDI advertising campaign) New York 1977-78.

Du/von Hapsburg, p. 61, reproduced.

Vogue Italia/Clay, p. 130, reproduced in color.

John Russell, "Easter Beyond the Egg," *The New York Times*, March 22, 1978, reproduced p. C1.

5. CHANTICLEER EGG

10-7/8 in./277 mm.
12-5/8 in./320 mm open.
MARKS: *FABERGÉ, 56 kokoshnik JL, MP* on top edge of base; *MP kokoshnik* on lower edge. (Perchin).
CASE: Fitted brown oak, lined with brown suede; 14-1/4 in./365 mm.; unstamped, probably LACLOCHE FRÈRES/15 Rue de la Paix/2 New Bond Street.
ACC. NO. FAB66005

Enamelled a dazzling translucent Cambridge blue on a guilloche gold ground, this monumental egg in the French neo-classical style is, after the Uspensky Cathedral Egg of 1904, the largest of the Imperial Eggs known today. The egg is applied with chased green-gold swags pendant from red-gold ribbons encircling the grille top. A band of foliage about the center is not chased in such high relief as the swags and is set with a central band of pearls. A similar band of pearls decorates the bezel of the white enamel dial of the clock, the hands of which are of pierced gold. The numerals are painted in blue enamel and the face is further embellished with foliate borders in green enamel. The fluted gold shaft joining the egg and the large gold base is applied with green-gold husks on a white enamel ground. The shaped octagonal base has four large panels of blue enamel applied with devices in two-color gold symbolizing the Arts and Sciences. These panels are bordered horizontally with gold-rimmed translucent white enamel bands mounted with chased two-color-gold foliage and rosettes. Vertically they are separated by rectangular panels also enamelled translucent white and chased with tassels and acanthus foliage in red gold overlaid with finely chased green-gold laurel swags. The grille at the top of the clock conceals the "surprise"—a gold chanticleer enamelled in yellow, blue and green and set with rose diamonds, which emerges automatically, bobbing its head and flapping its wings while crowing the hour. At the back of the egg is a pierced grille and two swivelling rosettes hiding the winding mechanism which is worked with a large silver key.

(Appendix D for details of egg, mechanism and key).

PROVENANCE

Presented by Czar Nicholas II to his mother, Maria Feodorovna, c. 1903.

Hammer Galleries, New York.

Maurice Sandoz, Switzerland.

A La Vieille Russie, New York.

Lansdell K. Christie, Long Island.

EXHIBITIONS

"Presentation of Imperial Russian Easter Gifts by Carl Fabergé," Hammer Galleries, New York, 1939, unnumbered, described and reproduced in the catalogue.

Corcoran 1961, no. 2, catalogue pp. 8, 14, 25, reproduced in color p. 8.

ALVR 1961, catalogue no. 295, pp. 16, 94, reproduced in color opposite.

Metropolitan 1962-66, no. L.62.8.2.

NYCC/Waterfield 1973, no. 3, catalogue pp. 4, 30, detail reproduced, reproduced in color p. 31.

V & A/Snowman 1977, no. L2, catalogue p. 71, reproduced in color p. 81.

REFERENCES

Alfred Chapuis, *Les Oeufs de Pâques de Carl Fabergé*, date unknown, pp.396-97.

Snowman 1953, p. 89, reproduced with details nos. 312-315.

Alfred Chapuis and Edmond Droz, *Automata*, London and Neuchâtel, 1958, Plate XI, reproduced, details figs. 280-284. (First published Neuchâtel 1949).

"Notes," *The Metropolitan Museum of Art Bulletin*, April 1962, p. 264, reproduced.

Rosine Rauol, "Fabergé at the Metropolitan Museum," *Apollo*, June 1962, p. 307, reproduced fig. 4.

Jeanne Horn, *Hidden Treasure, How and Where to Find It*, New York, 1962, no. 1, p. 19, reproduced.

Snowman 1962/64, p. 94, reproduced in color Plate LXXVI, details nos. 343-45.

Great Private Collections/Snowman, p. 241, reproduced in color.

Metropolitan Bulletin/McNab Dennis, pp. 241-2, reproduced no. 23.

New Yorker, July 8, 1967, p. 65, reproduced in color.

FORBES, August 1, 1967, p. 40, reproduced in color.

Louise Bruner, "Fabulous Fabergé Easter Eggs," *The Blade Sunday Magazine*, April 14, 1968, pp. 2, 9, reproduced in color front cover, reproduced p. 2.

"Splendors of the Court," *Horizon Book of Russia*, New York, 1970, p. 169 reproduced.

Rosemary Disney, *The Splendid Art of Decorating Eggs*, New York, 1972, Plate XXI, reproduced in color.

"Fabergé Show," *The Village Voice*, May 3, 1973, p. 46.

Newsweek/Douglas, p. 85, reproduced in color p. 84.

Rita Reif, "Antiques: Russian Art," *New York Times*, May 25, 1974, p. 26.

Villager/Sears, p. 3.

Helen Harris, "The Russian Antique—An Exercise in Rarity," *Town & Country*, May 1976, p. 166.

Agnes Clark, "Imperial Russia's Objects of Art," *The Boston Globe*, June 13, 1976, reproduced.

"Create an Elegant Easter from a Simple Egg," *Weight Watchers*, March 1977, p. 25, reproduced in color.

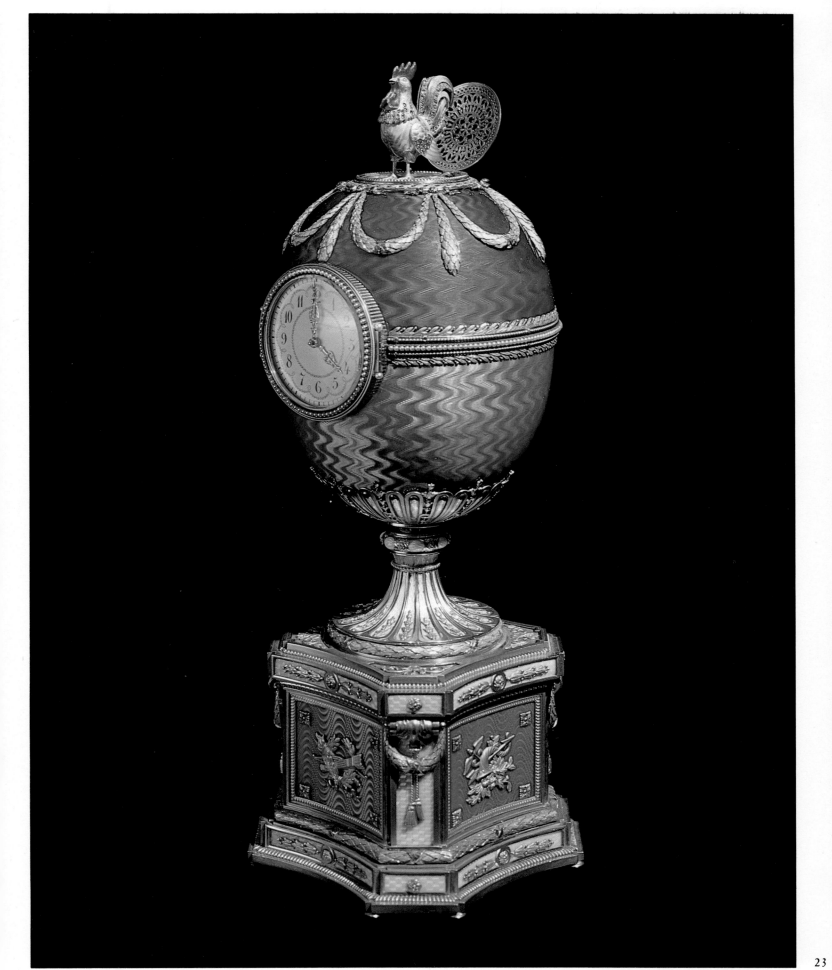

5. Chanticleer Egg, open (reduced 15%)

V & A Coming Events, London, May-June 1977, front cover, reproduced in color.

Nineteenth Century/Snowman, p. 52, reproduced in color.

Kate Dyson, "Fabergé Show Intrigues London Crowds," *Antique Monthly*, August 1977, p. 13A, reproduced in color.

N.Y. Times/Reif, p. C17.

Du/von Hapsburg, p. 79, reproduced twice, p. 78, detail reproduced in color.

The Soho Weekly News, March 23, 1978, center spread, no. 4, reproduced.

6. FIFTEENTH ANNIVERSARY EGG

5-1/8 in./132 mm.

6-1/4 in./160 mm.

MARKS: *FABERGÉ* twice in blue enamel on ribbons under the dates.

CASE: Original fitted velvet-covered egg shape; 8-3/8 in./213 mm.; lining stamped in black *Eagle/FABERGÉ/St. Petersburg/Moscow London.*

ACC. NO. FAB66023

The gold shell of the egg is chased and enamelled with a trellis of green laurel set with rose diamond ties at the intersections. It is divided into eighteen panels in three tiers, each set with scenes from the life of Nicholas II and portraits of him and his family painted on ivory by Vassily Zuiev framed behind crystals. The portraits of the Czar, Czarina, their four daughters and their son are framed in rose diamonds on panels of translucent pale pinkish-blue enamel. The larger panels intersecting them vertically are (from top to bottom and rotating clockwise after the portrait of the Czar):

The Alexander III Museum;

The procession to Uspensky Cathedral;

The opening of the Alexander III bridge in Paris;

The Huis ten Bosch, The Hague;

The reception for the members of the First State Duma at the Winter Palace, St. Petersburg;

The unveiling of the monument commemorating Bicentenary of the Battle of Poltava;

The unveiling of the statue of Peter the Great at Riga;

The moment of Coronation;

The removal of the remains of the Saint Serafim Sarovski.

Below the portraits of the Czar and Czarina are the dates 1894 and 1911 roses and blue ribbons, each signed: Fabergé. The top of the egg has the Czarina's cypher in black on gold beneath a table diamond, the base is set with a rose diamond.

On a gold stand made before 1916.

The Czar is wearing a Guard's uniform and the ribbon of the Order of St. Andrew. The names and dates of birth of his children are Olga (1895), Tatiana (1897), Marie (1899), Anastasia (1901) and Alexis (1904).

6. *Fifteenth Anniversary Egg*

The Alexander III Museum was in St. Petersburg. Nicholas II was present at the opening of the Alexander III bridge in Paris: It crosses the Seine between the Place Concorde and Les Invalides. The Huis ten Bosch was where the first 'peace' conference took place in May 1899. The conference resulted from a note to European Governments from Nicholas II in 1898 lamenting the arms race: the participants were to agree on rules of warfare and establish a permanent court of arbitration, which still exists today. The first State Duma was elected in May 1906, but their demands for universal suffrage, radical land reform, release of prisoners, and the election of ministers acceptable to the Duma was intolerable to the Czar, who dismissed them. Poltava is the chief city of the rich wheat-growing area of the Ukraine. Here Peter the Great defeated Charles XII of Sweden in 1709. His decisive battle gained him control over the Balkan states. Serafim Sarovski was the last saint to be canonized in Russia.

Zuiev also painted the miniatures for the Romanov Tercentenary Egg of 1913 now in the Armory Museum, The Kremlin, Moscow, and the Grisaille Egg of 1914, as well as the miniature of Nicholas II on the Nephrite Box (Catalogue no. 63).

(Appendix D for details of miniatures, signatures and stand).

PROVENANCE
Presented by Czar Nicholas II to his wife, Alexandra Feodorovna, 1911.
A La Vieille Russie, New York.

EXHIBITIONS
"In the Presence of Kings," The Metropolitan Museum of Art, New York, June-September, 1967, No. L.67.31.2.
NYCC/Waterfield 1973, no. 4, catalogue pp. 3, 32-34, reproduced in color p. 33, reproduced p. 35.
V & A/Snowman 1977, no. L7, catalogue pp.72-3, reproduced three times.

REFERENCES
"Easter Eggs, Gifts of the Sovereign Emperor to the Sovereign Empress Alexandra Feodorovna," *Town & Country, The Journal of Elegant Living*, Petrograd, April 1, 1916, p. 6, reproduced.
Snowman 1953, pp.94-5, reproduced no. 330.
Snowman 1962/64, p. 101, reproduced no. 365, details no. 366.
New Yorker, March 18, 1967, p. 160, reproduced in color.
FORBES, May 1, 1967, p. 62, reproduced in color.
Robert Massey, "Nicholas and Alexandra," *Reader's Digest Condensed Books*, Autumn, 1964, p. 358, reproduced in color, individual miniatures reproduced in color, pp. 342, 345, 356, 360, 381, 383, 398, 406, 424, 432, 450, 469.
E. M. Halliday, *Russia in Revolution*, New York, 1967, p. 63, reproduced in color, p. 62.
"Scene and Not Herd," *Harper's Bazaar*, 1967, p. 132, reproduced.
Louise Bruner, "Fabulous Fabergé Easter Eggs," *The Blade Sunday Magazine*, April 14, 1968, p. 8, reproduced in color.

"The Egg . . . Symbolizes the Fertility of Spring in Season of Joyous Rebirth," syndicated by Gannett News Service, April 19, 1973, reproduced.
Robert Carmell, "Solid Gold Easter Eggs Fit for a Czar," *Times Union*, Albany, April 26, 1973, reproduced.
"Fabergé Show," *The Village Voice*, May 3, 1973, p. 46.
"A Fabergé Imperial Egg for Your Rich Maiden Aunt," *Town & Country*, December 1973, reproduced in color.
Betty Jo Shirley, "The Great Easter Egg Hunt," *Coast*, April 7, 1974, reproduced on front cover and on contents page.
Villager/Sears, p. 3, reproduced.
Home News/Cook, p.C1, reproduced.
Nineteenth Century/Snowman, p. 50 reproduced.
N.Y. Times/Reif, p. C17.
Du/von Hapsburg, p. 82.
Vogue Italia/Clay p. 130, reproduced in color.

7. ORANGE TREE EGG

10-1/2 in./267 mm.
11-3/4 in./300 mm. open.
Key: 2-1/2 in./63 mm.
MARKS: Engraved *FABERGÉ, 1911* on front bottom edge of tub; scratched *2990, kmmm11.*
CASE: Fitted red morocco; 12-7/8 in./327 mm.; exterior stamped in gold *A.G.H.*
ACC. NO. FAB65002

The tree has four main branches which rise from the naturalistically chased gold trunk and divide into smaller branches to hold the nephrite leaves, each finely carved with veining and with a socket at the back into which fits the gold twig. The flowers of white enamel have diamond centers; the buds, rose diamonds; and the fruits, citrines, amethysts, pale rubies and champagne diamonds. The top third of the tree contains the movement for the singing bird which emerges from the top of the tree by pressing a jewelled fruit. It then moves its head from side to side, flaps its wings and opens its beak. The leaves fit together to disguise the opening when it is closed. The tub is of white agate overlaid by a gold trelliswork enriched with enamelled green swags set with cabochon rubies, and pearl finials at the corners. The whole stands upon a nephrite base, the nephrite posts at the corners applied with spiral bands of gold foliage and connected by free-swinging swags of enamelled-green husks and pearls.

A mechanical tubbed orange tree by the eighteenth-century jeweller Richard of Paris was formerly in the collection of the Earl of Rosebury (Sale: Sotheby Parke Bernet, Mentmore Towers, May 18, 1977, reproduced in color in the catalogue). A similar piece probably provided the inspiration for Fabergé's twentieth-century fantasy. As is so often the case with Fabergé's "borrowings" from the past, the resultant work is more neatly balanced stylistically and superior technically.

(Appendix D for tree by Richard).

7. Orange Tree Egg (reduced 11%)

PROVENANCE

Presented by Czar Nicholas II to his mother, Maria Feodorovna, 1911.

Wartski, London.

A. G. Hughes, England.

Arthur E. Bradshaw.

W. Magalow.

Maurice Sandoz, Switzerland.

A La Vieille Russie, New York.

Mildred Kaplan, New York.

EXHIBITIONS

"The Exhibition of Russian Art," 1 Belgrave Square, London, June 4-July 13, 1935, no. 582, catalogue p. 110.

ALVR 1961, no. 294, catalogue pp. 16, 92, reproduced p. 93.

ALVR 1968, no. 369, catalogue p. 138, reproduced in color opposite.

"Every One a Gem," *The New York Sunday News,* January 19, 1969, p. 23, reproduced in color.

Esquire, p. 139, reproduced in color.

"An Easter Fantasy: Fabergé Eggs," *Architectural Digest,* p. 56, reproduced in color p. 55.

Rita Reif, "Antiques: Russian Art," *New York Times,* May 25, 1974, p. 26.

Villager/Sears, p. 5.

Helen Harris, "The Russian Antiques—An Exercise in Rarity," *Town Country,* p. 165.

Home News/Cook, p. C2, reproduced twice.

Kate Dyson, "Fabergé Show Intrigues London Crowds," *Antique Monthly,* August 1977, p. A1, reproduced in color.

N.Y. Times/Reif, p. C17.

Du/von Hapsburg, p. 80, reproduced in color p. 81.

Palm Beach Life/Watts p. 38, reproduced in color p. 39.

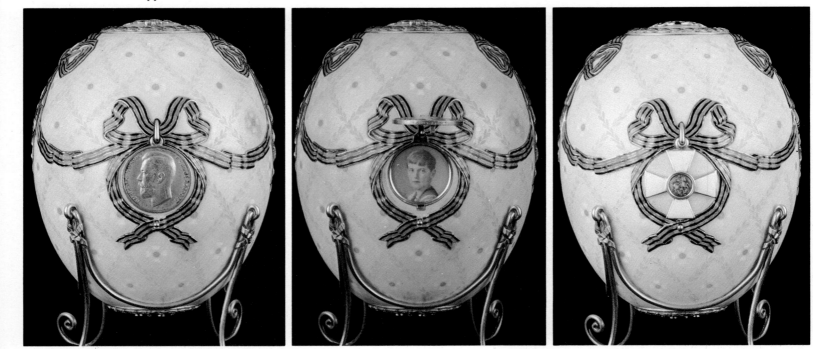

NYCC/Waterfield 1973, no. 5, catalogue pp. 3, 8, 11, 36, detail reproduced, reproduced in color p. 37.

V & A/Snowman 1977, no. L4, catalogue pp. 71-72, reproduced in color p. 81.

REFERENCES

H. C. Bainbridge, "Russian Imperial Easter Gifts, the Work of Carl Fabergé," *The Connoisseur,* May 1934, p. 304, reproduced p. 305 no. IX.

Snowman 1953, pp. 96-97, reproduced no. 334, detail reproduced no. 335.

Alfred Chapuis and Edmond Droz, *Automata,* Neuchâtel and New York, 1958, p. 205, reproduced in color IX, detail reproduced fig. 250 (first published in Neuchâtel in 1949).

Jeanne Horn, *Hidden Treasure, How and Where to Find It,* New York, 1962, p. 6, reproduced in color Plate III.

Snowman 1962/64, p. 102, reproduced in color Plate LXXVIII, detail reproduced no. 363.

New Yorker, June 3, 1967, p. 50, reproduced in color.

FORBES, June 15, 1967, p. 70, reproduced in color.

Louise Bruner, "Fabulous Fabergé Easter Eggs," *The Blade Sunday Magazine,* April 14, 1968, p. 9, reproduced in color p. 10.

8. *CROSS OF ST. GEORGE EGG*

3-5/16 in./90 mm.

4-1/8 in./105 mm. with stand.

MARKS: Engraved *FABERGÉ* on medallion edge.

CASE: Original fitted velvet-covered egg shape; 7-1/4 in./184 mm.; stamped in gold *Eagle* (wings stylized to form a circle around other wording)/*K. FABERGÉ/Petrograd Moscow/Odessa London.*

ACC. NO. FAB76010

Although less extravagant and perhaps less ingenious than its predecessors the simple silver egg commemorating the recent presentation of the Cross of the Order of St. George to Nicholas II still reflects Fabergé's unerring sense of design. Enamelled matt opalescent white over ground trellised with laurel garlands which form frames for paintings of the St. George Cross, the shell is further decorated with gold ribbons enamelled in the Order's colors, black and orange, and seemingly pendant from the raised chased silver wreath surrounding the Dowager Em-

8. Cross of St. George Egg

press' similarly executed cypher. The base is likewise applied with the date. The surprises are contained behind two medallions "tied" with bows of enamelled ribbon to the egg. Behind the badge of the Order of St. George a miniature of the Czar is revealed when a small button below the badge is depressed. A miniature of the Czarevitch, who also was awarded a lower grade of the Order of St. George, is similarly revealed from behind a silver St. George Medal depicting Nicholas II when a second button is pushed. This austerity egg of silver was the last in the series of Imperial Eggs to be delivered; it was also the only egg to leave Russia in the possession of its original recipient. Thanking her son after that last untroubled Easter, the Dowager Empress wrote:

Christ has indeed arisen! I kiss you three times and thank you with all my heart for your dear cards and lovely egg with miniatures, which dear old Fabergé brought himself. It is beautiful.
It is so sad not to be together. I wish you, my dear darling Nicky, with all my heart all the best things and success in everything.
—Your fondly loving old
Mama.

It was the Dowager Empress' separation from the Czar and his family which was to make possible her eventual escape from Russia. The actual Cross of the Order of St. George which was presented to the Czar was found, after the murder of him and his family, hidden in the bathroom of the Impatiev House.

The Order of St. George was created by Catherine the Great in 1769 to be awarded by the army and not the sovereign for bravery in war. ·

(Appendix D for details of cypher, date and stand).

PROVENANCE
Presented by Czar Nicholas II to his mother, Maria Feodorovna, 1916.
Grand Duchess Xenia Alexandrovna, Windsor, her daughter.
A La Vieille Russie, New York.
EXHIBITIONS
"The Exhibition of Russian Art," Belgrave Square, London, June 4-July 13, 1935, no. 560, catalogue p. 108, reproduced.
V & A/Snowman 1977, no. L12, catalogue p. 74, reproduced.
REFERENCES
E. J. Bing (ed), *The Secret Letters of the Last Tsar*, New York, 1938.
Snowman 1953, p. 103, reproduced no. 354.
Snowman 1962/64, p. 109, reproduced Plate 385 with five details.
Howard Ricketts, *Antique Gold and Enamelware in Color*, New York, 1971, p. 106, reproduced in color.
FORBES, February 1, 1977, p. 74, reproduced in color.
Home News/Cook p. C1, reproduced p. C2.
Rita Reif, "If It's by Fabergé, Forbes Finds Putting Eggs in One Basket Pays Off," *Trenton Times*, April 26, 1978, reproduced with description (syndicated text of *N.Y. Times*/Reif).

9. DUCHESS OF MARLBOROUGH EGG

9-1/4 in./235 mm.
MARKS: *56, kokoshnik JL, FABERGÉ* on bottom; *MP, kokoshnik JL* on side panel border; *MP kokoshnik, MP* on front panel border; *MP* inside handle; *kokoshnik JL* on handle; inscribed in Roman script *K. Fabergé.* (Perchin).
CASE: Original fitted hollowood; 10 in./255 mm.; lining stamped in black *Eagle/FABERGÉ/S. Petersburg/Moscow Odessa.*
ACC. NO. FAB65001

The gold egg of pink enamel on a guilloche ground is bisected with a revolving white enamel band at the center set with rose-diamond Roman numerals and seed pearl borders. About the gadrooned stem is entwined a rose-diamond encrusted serpent the pointed tongue of which indicates the hour. The upper part of the egg is applied with floral swags in four-color gold suspended from rose-diamond ties and terminates in a rose-diamond-set red-gold pineapple finial. The handles rising from goat-head masks are also of red gold and are ornamented with chased green-gold foliage. The base is decorated with panels of translucent white enamel, one of which is applied with the monogram CM surmounted by an English ducal coronet in rose diamonds. The monogram is repeated in reverse making an almost indecipherable arabesque of rose diamonds. The other two panels are decorated with amatory trophies in four-color gold, and the smaller pink panels between are applied with chased green-gold foliage.

This egg was made for the Duchess of Marlborough, the former Consuelo Vanderbilt, during the Marlborough's visit to Russia in 1902. It is very similar to the smaller Serpent Clock Egg presented to Czarina Maria Feodorovna either by her son or her husband prior to 1896. In addition to minor decorative variations, the earlier egg is enamelled translucent navy blue. Both eggs are based on works by goldsmiths of an earlier century.

(Appendix D for detail of back and Imperial Serpent Clock Egg).

PROVENANCE
The Duchess of Marlborough, Blenheim Palace (Sale, in aid of a hospital at Vincennes, "Grand Prix Day," the Cercle Interallié, Paris, c. 1926. The Duchess was divorced in 1920 and married to Jacques Balsan on July 4, 1921. The Balsans lived in Paris).
Mme. Ganna Walska (Sale: Parke-Bernet, New York, May 14-15, 1965, Lot 326, catalogue p. 50, reproduced twice p. 51. Mme. Walska was a singer in the 1920s and the divorced wife of Harold Fowler McCormick).
EXHIBITION
NYCC/Waterfield 1973, no. 7, catalogue pp. 3, 8, 40, reproduced in color p. 41.
REFERENCES
Consuelo Vanderbilt Balsan, *The Glitter and the Gold*, New York, 1952, p. 252.

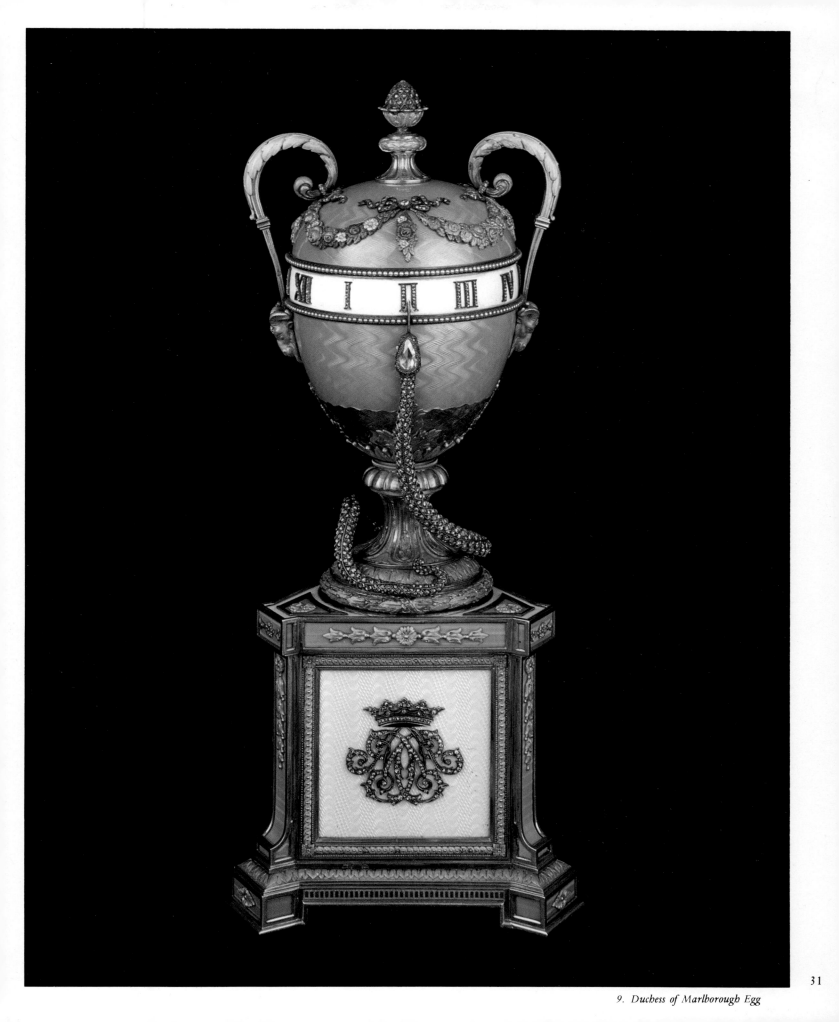

9. *Duchess of Marlborough Egg*

"Parke-Bernet Sales—A $50,000 Clock," *New York Times*, May 16, 1965.

"International Sale Room," *The Connoisseur* (American Edition) August 1965, p. 268, reproduced.

"Auction Prices Last Season," *Antiques*, August 1965, p. 172.

FORBES, March 1, 1968, p. 37, reproduced in color.

Home News/Cook. p. C2.

10. KELCH HEN EGG

3-1/4 in./84 mm.
3-5/8 in./92 mm. high with stand.
HEN: 1-3/8 in./35 mm.
EASEL: 1-7/8 in./56 mm.
MARKS: *56 kokoshnik, MP, ET* on top rim; *FABERGÉ, MP, 56 kokoshnik, ET* on bottom rim; *ET, ET* on easel strut. (Perchin).
CASE: Original fitted hollowood; 4-1/2 in./107mm.; lid lining stamped in gold *Eagle/FABERGÉ/St. Petersburg/Moscow.*
ACC. NO. FAB66006

The gold egg is enamelled a lustrous strawberry and opens in half lengthwise. The rim is set with rose diamonds and two table-cut diamonds covering the date 1898 and a portrait of Nicholas II. The partially filled interior is enamelled opaque glossy white to resemble the white of an egg, and the matt yellow enamelled yolk opens to reveal a suede liner fitted to hold a gold hen. The hen is naturalistically enamelled in brown with touches of white and is hinged at the tail to open horizontally. The surprise contained within is a gold easel set with rose diamonds, the three struts of which are hinged at the center to fold behind, as is the diamond and ruby-set cresting. The frame now contains a portrait of the Czarevitch Alexis wearing the uniform of the 4th (Imperial Family) Rifle Battalion of Guards. This egg is a more fanciful and sophisticated working out of the same motif used in the First Imperial Egg (catalogue no. 1).

The detachable six-footed vari-colored gold stand embellished with diamond-set floral swags was ordered for the egg by H. M. King Farouk of Egypt.

Kenneth Snowman recalls the initials BK and not the portrait beneath the diamond at the end when he examined this piece at the Corcoran, 1961, but Mrs. Jessie McNab Dennis reports that the portrait had been substituted before the loan to The Metropolitan Museum in 1962. There is a photograph in the Hammer Galleries' catalogue of 1939 but it does not show that side of the egg: the photograph does however portray the easel without the portrait of the Czarevitch. A similar egg of carved lapis lazuli mounted in gold is in the Cleveland Museum of Art, India Early Minshall Collection.

(Appendix D for details of egg open, stand and Lapis Lazuli Egg).

PROVENANCE
Presented by Alexander Ferdinandovitch Kelch to his wife, the former Barbara Bazanov, 1898. Mrs. Kelch owned gold mines in Siberia as well as real estate.
Hammer Galleries, New York.
H. M. King Farouk (Sale, by order of the Egyptian Government: Sotheby & Co., Cairo, March 10-13, 17-20, 1954, Lot 165, catalogue p. 33, reproduced Plate 6).
Lansdell K. Christie, Long Island.

EXHIBITIONS
"Presentation of Imperial Russian Easter Gifts by Carl Fabergé," Hammer Galleries, New York, 1939, unnumbered, described and reproduced in the catalogue.
Corcoran 1961, no. 3, catalogue p. 26, reproduced in color p. 21.
Metropolitan 1962-66, no. L.62.8.3.
NYCC/Waterfield, 1973, no. 6, catalogue pp. 13, 38, reproduced in color p. 39.

REFERENCES
Snowman 1953, p. 105, reproduced no. 357.
Snowman 1962/64, p. 111, reproduced in color Plate LXXXII.
Great Private Collections/Snowman, p. 243, reproduced in color p. 242.
Metropolitan Bulletin/McNab Dennis, p. 242, reproduced no. 26.
Henry H. Hawley, *Fabergé and His Contemporaries*, Cleveland, 1973, p. 72.
FORBES, May 1, 1968, p. 67, reproduced in color.
Esquire, p. 139, reproduced in color p. 138.
FORBES, July 15, 1973, p. 76, reproduced in color.
"An Easter Fantasy: Fabergé Eggs," *Architectural Digest*, p. 56, reproduced in color p. 55.
Home News/Cook, p. C2, reproduced.
Du/von Hapsburg, p. 87, reproduced.
Jean Nichols, "The Arts . . . and You," *News-Virginian*, Waynesboro, April 19, 1978, reproduced.

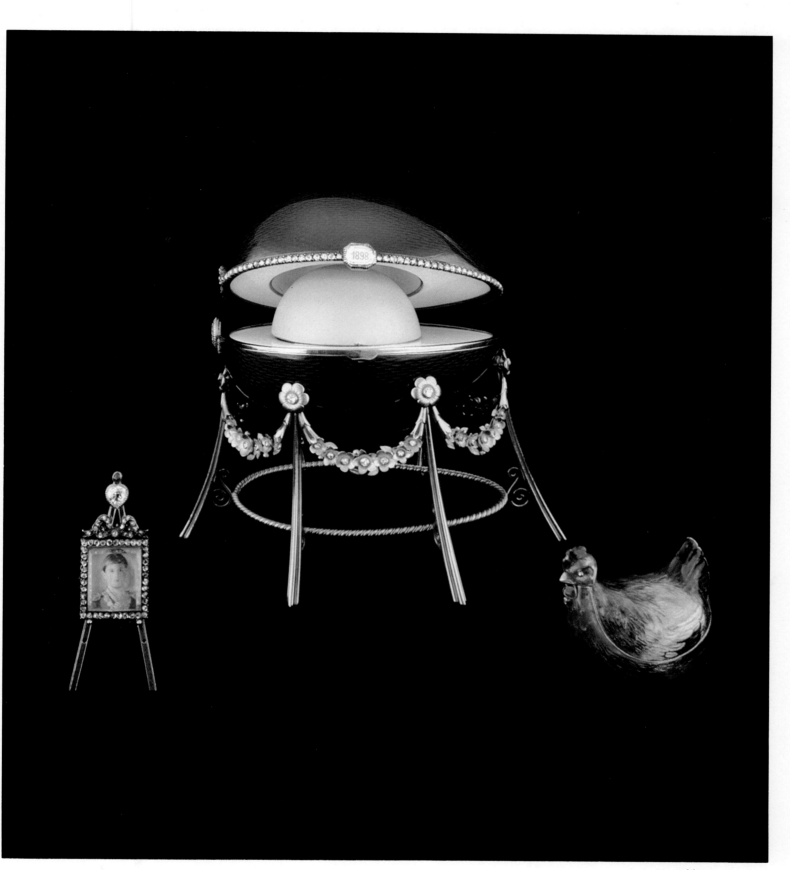

10. Kelch Hen Egg

11. RABBIT EGG

2 in./50 mm.
3-3/8 in./86 mm. with stand.
RABBIT: 1-1/8 in./38 mm.
MARKS: *MP, 56 kokoshnik* on chased band. (Perchin).
CASE: Fitted hollywood; 4-3/4 in./120 mm.; lining stamped in gold *A La Vieille Russie /781 Fifth Avenue/New York.*
ACC. NO. FAB66015

A silver-gilt egg enamelled a translucent yellow and applied with foliage rim chased in green gold. Inside is a gold panel notched to resemble grass and with a sunken division made to contain the pink chalcedony rabbit, the eyes set with olivines.

On a gold stand set with an Elizabeth I ruble dated 1756 and enamelled red.

PROVENANCE
A La Vieille Russie, New York.
Lansdell K. Christie, Long Island.
EXHIBITIONS
Metropolitan 1962-68, no. L.62.8.130.
NYCC/Waterfield 1973, no. 9, catalogue p. 42, reproduced in color p. 43.
REFERENCES
FORBES, August 1, 1968, p. 37, reproduced in color.
The New York Cultural Center—Members Calendar, Spring 1973, reproduced.
Betty Jo Shirley, "The Great Easter Egg Hunt," *Coast*, April 7, 1974, p. 83, reproduced.
Home News/Cook, p. C1, reproduced.
Vogue Italia/Clay, p. 131, reproduced in color.

12. HOOF EGG

2-1/8 in./55 mm.
3-1/4 in./83 mm. open.
MARKS: *FABERGÉ, MP, 56 anchors* on miniature back; *MP* on hoof; *MP* on hoof; *MP, 56* on hoof; scratched *4845.* (Perchin).
CASE: Fitted black morocco; 4-1/8 in./105; lining stamped in gold *A La Vieille Russie/781 Fifth Avenue/New York.*
ACC. NO. FAB66003

The bowenite egg is applied with swags of laurel chased in green gold and bound with red-gold ties, suspended from rose diamond knots of ribbon, cabochon rubies and pearls, on four gold feet formed as hooves. The center is cut lengthwise to contain a circular gold frame on a swivel hinge: this contains a miniature portrait of Alexandra Feodorovna in Court Robes wearing the chain for the Order of St. Andrew and the Kokoshnik diadem.

PROVENANCE
A La Vieille Russie, New York.
EXHIBITION
NYCC/Waterfield 1973, no. 9, catalogue p. 42, reproduced in color p. 43.
REFERENCES
FORBES, September 1, 1971, p. 34, reproduced in color.
Home News/Cook, p. C1, reproduced.

11. Rabbit Egg

12. Hoof Egg (enlarged 30%)

13. Egg Bonbonnière

13. EGG BONBONNIÈRE

1-7/8in./48mm.
MARKS: *JL kokoshnik 88, HW* inside lid; *JL kokoshnik 88, HW* inside bottom; *HW, 56 kokoshnik JL* on rim; scratched *3139, 3139.* (Wigström).
CASE: Blue silk egg shape; 2-7/8 in./75mm.; lining stamped in gold L. DESOUTTER/from Le Roy et Fils/4 Hanover Street/London.
ACC. NO. FAB65007

Of silver-gilt enamelled with panels in a translucent white painted with wintry foliage beneath the final layer of enamel, and applied with rubies within chased foliage: also with smaller pale blue panels of enamel applied with gold trelliswork set with diamonds at the intersections. Between are applied laurel swags of chased gold pendant from cabochon ruby centers. The hinged cover is applied with red-gold knots of ribbon, green-gold foliage and rose diamonds.

Three sets of three pinks hold the florettes and trelliswork, and also the knots of ribbon on the cover, which are drilled through the body of the egg. This is a difficult technical operation which was probably carried out in the same manner as was used for the Coronation box (Catalogue no. 61).

PROVENANCE
L. Desoutter, London.
Mrs. L. Turnbull, England.
Anon. Sale: Christie's, London, December 8, 1965, Lot 7, reproduced in catalogue.
EXHIBITION
NYCC/Waterfield 1973, no. 10, catalogue p. 44, reproduced in color p. 45.
REFERENCES
Christie's Bi-Centenary Review of the Year, London 1966, p. 156, reproduced.
FORBES, February 1, 1969, p. 46, reproduced in color.
Barbara Goldsmith, *The Straw Man*, New York, 1975, reproduced in color on front cover.
Vogue Italia/Clay, p. 129, reproduced in color.

14. EGG SCENT FLAÇON

1-1/4in./32mm.
MARKS: *HW, 56* on loop. (Wigström).
CASE: Fitted brown morocco; 2-3/8 in./60 mm.
ACC. NO. FAB66010

The gold egg is enamelled in blue and applied with gold swags which hang from rose diamonds. The detachable screw base is set with a moonstone.

PROVENANCE
Lansdell K. Christie, Long Island.
EXHIBITIONS
Corcoran 1961, no. 52, catalogue pp. 43-44.
Metropolitan 1962-66, no. L.62.8.52.
NYCC/Waterfield 1973, no. 43, reproduced in color p. 95.
REFERENCES
Great Private Collections/Snowman, p. 247, reproduced in color p. 246.

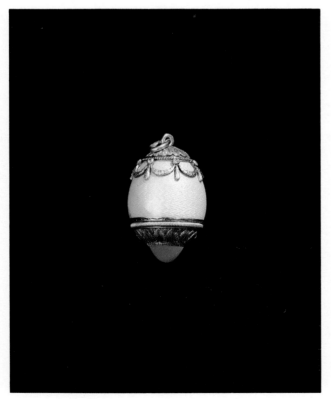

14. Egg Scent Flaçon

Metropolitan Bulletin/McNab Dennis, p. 242 reproduced no. 24.
FORBES, June 15, 1972, p. 64, reproduced in color.
Vogue Italia/Clay, p. 131, reproduced in color.

15-48. MINIATURE EGGS

1-1/8 in./30 mm. largest.
5/8 in./16 mm. smallest.
MARKS: on loops as noted individually.
ACC. NO. (15-27) FAB66011

Thirty-four jelly-bean-sized eggs executed in gold, enamel, semi-precious and precious stones. Like their larger counterparts, these egg charms or pendants would have been exchanged on Easter with the greeting, "Christ is Risen."

PROVENANCE
(15-27) Lansdell K. Christie, Long Island.

EXHIBITIONS
(15-27) Corcoran 1961, no. 77 a-m, catalogue p. 50.
(15-27) Metropolitan 1962-66, no. L.62.8.72 a-m.
(15-32, 34-45, 47) NYCC/Waterfield 1973, no. 11A-CM, pp. 46-48, reproduced p. 47, reproduced in color, p. 49. Exact letter references included in parentheses following individual descriptions.

REFERENCES
(15-32, 34-46, 47) *FORBES*, June 1, 1970, p. 41, reproduced in color.
(14, 16, 17, 19, 20, 22, 23, 28-31, 35, 37, 38, 40, 43) *Newsweek*/Douglas, p. 85, reproduced in color p. 84.

15. Gold egg enamelled with a red cross on a white ground. The Czarina and her daughters all worked for the Red Cross after the outbreak of World War I. A large amount of the personal fortune of the Imperial family was spent supporting the Red Cross and other war efforts. (C.G.). MARKS: *56*.

16. Gold egg enamelled on one side with the Romanov eagle on a golden yellow ground and on the other with bands of white blue and red, the colors of Imperial Russia. (C.H.). MARKS: *56, FA* (Afanassiev).

17. Gold egg enamelled lime green and chased with the Cross of St. George. (C.F.). MARKS: *56,* another obscured.

18. Gold egg enamelled with the Union Jack on a white ground. (C.K.). MARKS: *56, JL, GL.* (Lundell).

19. Gold egg enamelled blue celeste and chased with a pair of anchors. (C.E.). MARKS: *56 JL, EK.* (Kollin).

20. Gold egg enamelled white and set with a square-cut ruby. (C.E.).

21. Purpurine egg surmounted by a miniature black-enamelled gold helmet of Her Imperial Majesty's Guard Lancers. From the helmet hangs a tassel of chased silver. (C.A.).

REFERENCE: *Metropolitan Bulletin*/McNab Dennis, p. 25, reproduced no. 25.

15-21. Miniature Eggs (clockwise from top left)

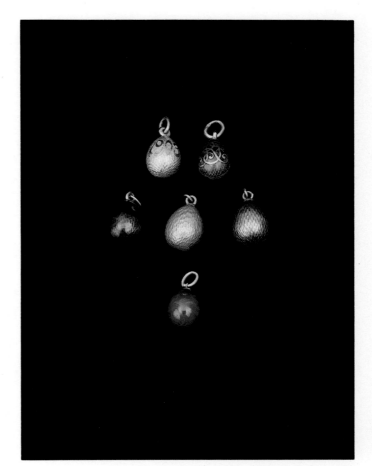

22-27. Miniature Eggs (clockwise from top left)

22. Gold egg enamelled yellow and chased with the monogram RF and the year 1903. (C.D.).

   MARKS: *ET on ring, 56, IO.* (Okerblom).

23. Gold egg enamelled green and chased with the monogram RF and the year 1900. (C.C.).

   MARKS: *AT on ring; ET AT.* (Tillander).

24. Gold egg enamelled gun-metal blue. (C.M.).

25. Gold egg enamelled royal blue. (C.L.).

26. Gold egg enamelled aubergine. (C.J.).

   MARKS: *56 anchors, BA.* (Aarne).

27. Gold egg enamelled green. (C.I.).

   MARKS: *BA, 56.* (Aarne).

28. Gold egg pavé-set with rose diamonds and emeralds. (G.).

   MARKS: *HW, anchors.* (Wigström).
   ACC. NO. FAB67003
   PROVENANCE: A La Vieille Russie, New York.

29. Nephrite egg with pavé-set rose diamond cap, the whole resembling an acorn. (Q.).

   MARKS: *HW, 56.* (Wigström).

30. Gold egg pavé-set with rubies. (F.).

   MARKS: *EK, 56 JL.* (Kollin).

31. Gold egg enamelled with a red cross on a white ground. (R.).

   MARKS: *56,* another partly obscured *A * H* (?) (Hollming?).
   The property of Mrs. Malcolm S. Forbes.
   PROVENANCE: A La Vieille Russie, New York.

32. Nephrite egg.

   MARKS: *KF, 56.*
   ACC. NO. FAB68003a
   PROVENANCE: Anon. Sale: Christie's, London, April 2, 1968, Lot 78, catalogue p. 27; I. Freeman & Son, London and New York.

33. Gold egg enamelled white and chased with two waving ribbons terminating in drops of rose diamonds and rubies, the whole in the Art Nouveau taste.

   MARKS: *56,* obscured *MP* (?). (Perchin?).
   ACC. NO. FAB73007
   PROVENANCE: A La Vieille Russie, New York.

34. Small purpurine egg hanging from a miniature gold crown set with rubies and rose diamonds. (P.).

   MARKS: *OP, St. George 56* (Pihl).

28-34. Miniature Eggs (clockwise from top left)

35. Gold egg the white-enamelled lower half divided from the blue-enamelled cap by a castellated band of rose diamonds. (D.)

   MARKS: *AT, 56.* (Thielemann).
   ACC. NO. FAB66017
   PROVENANCE: Anna Lois Webber.

36. Gold egg enamelled with bands of white and set with a *saumon-fumé*-enamelled, rose-diamond-set crown. (E.).

   MARKS: *MP, 56 JL.* (Perchin).
   ACC. NO. FAB68004
   PROVENANCE: A La Vieille Russie, New York.

37. Gold egg, the green-enamelled lower half divided from the pink-enamelled cap by a castellated band on rose diamonds. (C.).

   MARKS: *AT.* (Thielemann).
   ACC. NO. FAB66018
   PROVENANCE: Anna Lois Webber.

38. Gold egg enamelled salmon-pink underpainted with wintry brown foliage, the whole surrounded by a band of rose diamonds. (A.).

   MARKS: *HW, 56 AP.* (Wigström).
   ACC. NO. FAB66022
   PROVENANCE: H. R. H. The Princess Royal (Sale: Christie's, London, June 28, 1966, catalogue p. 9, reproduced opposite); I. Freeman & Son, London and New York.

35-41. Miniature Eggs (clockwise from top left)

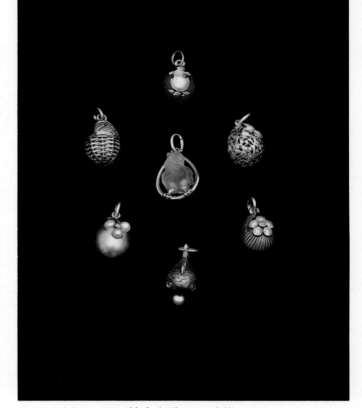

42-48. Miniature Eggs (clockwise from top left)

39. Gold egg enamelled auburn and chased with a *fleur-de-lys*. (L.).

    MARKS: *56, KF.*

40. Gold egg enamelled blue bisected with a segmented band in white applied with green-gold laurel swags caught in loops by red-gold flowers. (B.).

    MARKS: *56 JL, another obscured.*

41. Rhodonite egg surmounted with a miniature silver soldier and cannon.

    MARKS: partly obscured *AT* (?) (Thielemann?).

42. Gold egg of chased basket work, the top half chased with plants and a swan set with colored stones. (N.).

    MARKS: *HW, kokoshnik JL 56.*
    ACC. NO. FAB68002
    PROVENANCE: Anon. Sale: Christie's, London, April 2, 1968, Lot 77, catalogue p. 27; I. Freeman & Son, London and New York.

43. Gold egg enamelled with a chicken emerging from an egg on blue ground. (O.).

    MARKS: *KF, 56.*

44. Gold egg of open scroll work set with a crystal quatrefoil. (H.).

    MARKS: *A * H.* (Hollming).

45. Two color gold egg set with a cluster of pastes. The base is reeded. (I.).

    MARKS: *MP.* (Perchin).

46. The plump gold egg-shaped fish is oxidized to resemble gun metal except the fins and tail which remain gold. The open mouth holds a pearl and the eyes are set with cabochon rubies.

    MARKS: *56, KF.*
    ACC. NO. FAB75004
    PROVENANCE: Christie's, Geneva, November 11, 1975, Lot 179. A La Vieille Russie, New York.

47. Gold egg set with a flower comprised of a pearl trefoil centered with a rose diamond and chased gold stem. (K.)

    MARKS: *Anchors,* another partly obscured *WR* (?). (Reimar?).

48. A fluffy-looking chick carved from amethystine quartz and with rose-diamond eyes stands on gold legs within an egg-shaped perch.

    MARKS: *FA,* another obscured (Afanassiev).
    ACC. NO. FAB75005
    PROVENANCE: Christie's, Geneva, November 11, 1975, Lot 183. A La Vieille Russie, New York.

FANTASIES

While the Imperial Eggs are perhaps the ultimate fantasies created by the House of Fabergé, the other exercises of the genre would have ensured the firm's lasting reputation without the eggs. The brilliance of the execution of the miniature furniture, the engaging personalities of the hardstone carvings of man and beast and the almost impossible reality of the jewelled flowers have inspired the ultimate compliment — numerous imitations. While none has equalled the quality of the firm's goldsmithery and enamelling, some lapidaries of the last sixty years would most certainly have been welcomed into the firm by *Maître* Fabergé himself.

49. Dancing Moujik

50. Lancer

51. Helmet Seal

49. DANCING MOUJIK

5-1/4 in./132 mm.
CASE: Fitted green morocco; 6-3/4 in./72 mm.; lid lining stamped in gold *Crest/By Appointment to/H. M. The Queen/ Jewellers/WARTSKI/138 Regent St./London & Llandudno.*
ACC. NO. FAB66016

This figure of a peasant has a very animated stance which may indicate inebriation. He wears trousers of yellow chalcedony, purpurine tunic, and black marble boots and hat. His hands and face of pinkish agate, his hair and beard are cut from gray jasper, his eyes set with cabochon sapphires. A tasselled gold rope binds his waist.

Fabergé made a series of harstone figures recording the simple folk of Russia.

PROVENANCE
Anon. Sale: Sotheby & Co., London, July 3, 1961, Lot 179, reproduced in catalogue.
Lansdell K. Christie, Long Island.
EXHIBITIONS
Metropolitan 1962-66, no. L.62.8.51.
NYCC/Waterfield 1973, no. 22, catalogue p. 68, reproduced in color p. 69.
V & A/Snowman 1977, no. L13, catalogue p. 74.
REFERENCES
A.K. Snowman, "A Group of Virtuoso Pieces by Carl Fabergé," *The Connoisseur*, June 1962, p. 98, reproduced in color.
Great Private Collections/Snowman, p. 249, reproduced.
Metropolitan Bulletin/McNab Dennis, p. 236, reproduced no. 13.
FORBES, June 15, 1968, p. 52, reproduced in color.
N.Y. Times/Reif, p. C17, reproduced.

50. CAPTAIN OF THE 4th HARKOVSKY LANCERS

5 in./125 mm.
MARKS: *72 kokoshnik* on tunic strap; *88* on belt; *88 kokoshnik, HW,* engraved *1914-1915* on sword. (Wigström).
ACC. NO. FAB74004

He stands with his right arm akimbo, his left hand holding the gold hilt of his silver sword. His uniform is of lapis lazuli with buff agate facings, gold buttons and cross belt, silver epaulettes, and silver spurs to his long obsidian boots. His gold cap is enamelled black with yellow facings, gold Imperial Eagle and chin strap, silver tassel. His face and hands are of pink agate and his eyes are set with cabochon sapphires.

PROVENANCE
Anon. Sale: Sotheby & Co., London, March 29, 1965, Lot 174, catalogue p. 44, reproduced in color on frontispiece.
Anon. Sale: Sotheby Parke Bernet, New York, May 16-18, Lot 543, catalogue p. 140, reproduced in color p. 141.
A La Vieille Russie, New York.
REFERENCES
Art at Auction, 1973-74, New York and London, 1974, p. 258, reproduced in color.
FORBES, June 1, 1975, p. 55, reproduction in color.
N.Y. Times/Reif, p. C17.

52. Crystal Polar Bear (reduced 39%)

51. HELMET SEAL

1-1/2in./38mm.
ACC. NO. FAB74003

The conical seal of dark blue enamel is almost entirely enveloped by a miniature helmet of the Cavalier Guards in silver-gilt, surmounted by a chased silver Imperial Eagle on shaped cartouche, the front of the helmet has a silver Star of the Order of St. Andrew on blue and yellow enamel ground. The chased gold chin strap has an enamelled cockade hinge to one side. The white agate seal matrix, contained in narrow gold mount, is cut with a prancing horse.

(Appendix D for detail of matrix).

Anon. Sale: Sotheby Parke Bernet, New York, May 16-18, 1974, Lot 264, catalogue p. 16, reproduced.
A La Vieille Russie, New York.

52. CRYSTAL POLAR BEAR

3-1/2in./90mm.
6 in./154mm. including ice flow.
MARKS: A * H on pin joining bear to ice flow. (Hollming).
CASE: Fitted black morocco; 7-7/8 in./200 mm.; lining stamped in gold *A La Vieille Russie/785 Fifth Ave/New York.*
ACC. No. FAB66013

The figure is carved from a block of crystal, the eyes inset with rubies. It is fixed with silver screws to a crystal base molded to resemble an ice floe.

PROVENANCE
A La Vielle Russie, New York.
Lansdell K. Christie, Long Island.
EXHIBITIONS
Corcoran 1961, no. 94, catalogue p. 54.
Metropolitan 1962-66, no. L.62.8.94.
NYCC/Waterfield 1973, no. 23, catalogue p. 70, reproduced in color p. 71.
REFERENCES
Snowman 1962, no. 103, reproduced.
New Yorker, August 12, 1967, p. 54, reproduced in color.
FORBES, September 1, 1967, p. 65, reproduced in color.

53. PAIR OF ANGEL FISH

2-3/8in./62mm.
MARKS: *FA, FABERGÉ, alpha kokoshnik 56* on base. All on both. (Afanassiev).
ACC. NO. FAB76029

The angel fish are cut from a translucent agate, one with predominantly gray markings, the other with brown; both have cabochon ruby eyes and are held upright by seven slender fronds of seaweed in chased green gold. The oblong nephrite bases are mounted in red gold and rest on four bun feet.

PROVENANCE
Anon. Sale: Sotheby Parke Bernet, New York, December 10, 1976, no. 419, reproduced in color catalogue Plate VII.
A La Vieille Russie, New York.

43

53. Angel Fish

54. PINK RABBIT

1-1/8 in./28 mm.
CASE: Original fitted hollywood; 2-5/8 in./63 mm.; lid
lining stamped in gold *Eagle/FABERGÉ/St. Petersburg/
Moscow*.
ACC. NO. FAB65011

The carnelian body is finely carved to represent the
fur naturalistically, the eyes are set with rose
diamonds.

PROVENANCE
Czarina Maria Feodorovna.
Grand Duchess Xenia Alexandrovna, Windsor, her daugh-
ter.
Princess Andrew of Russia, her daughter-in-law (Sale:
Sotheby & Co., London, July 19, 1965, Lot 94, catalogue
p. 26, reproduced opposite).
I. Freeman & Son, London and New York.
EXHIBITION
NYCC/Waterfield 1973, no. 25, catalogue p. 72, repro-
duced p. 73.

54. Pink Rabbit

55. OWL SEAL

2-1/8 in./53 mm.
MARKS: HW, 56 on rim; scratched *18241, 18241*.
(Wigström).
ACC. NO. FAB68001

The owl is of white chalcedony, with ruby set eyes. It
is perched on a nephrite sphere which is applied and
set with a band of rose diamonds and four cabochon
rubies. The gadrooned base is of gold.

PROVENANCE
Anon. Sale: Parke-Bernet Galleries, New York, March 15,
1968, Lot 176, catalogue p. 44, reproduced opposite.
A La Vieille Russie, New York.
EXHIBITION
NYCC/Waterfield 1973, no. 24, catalogue p. 72, repro-
duced p. 73.
REFERENCES
Gérald Schurr, "Collecting Russian Jewelry," *Realités*
(American edition) November 1969, pp. 25-26, repro-
duced.
FORBES, October 1, 1972, p. 64, reproduced in color.

55. Owl Seal

56. WATERING CAN

4-1/8 in./105 mm.
MARKS: scratched *4709*.
CASE: Original fitted hollywood; 4-7/8 in./120 mm.; lid
lining stamped in gold *Eagle/K. FABERGÉ/St. Peters-
burg/Moscow*.
ACC. NO. FAB66008

The body and spout of the can are carved from a
single piece of nephrite. The handle is probably of
gold enamelled scarlet, the gold nozzle also
enamelled scarlet and set with rose diamonds.

A similar miniature nephrite watering can by Henrik Wigström in the collection of H. M. King
Farouk was sold by Sotheby & Co. in Cairo on March
10, 1954, no. 149 and is reproduced in the catalogue.

PROVENANCE
Mme. Elizabeth Balletta of the Imperial Michael Theater.
A La Vieille Russie, New York.
Lansdell K. Christie, Long Island.

EXHIBITIONS

Corcoran 1961, no. 11, catalogue p. 31, reproduced in color p. 12.

Metropolitan 1962-66, no. L.62.8.11.

ALVR 1961, no. 274, catalogue p. 80, reproduced p. 73.

ALVR 1968, no. 343, catalogue p. 130, reproduced.

NYCC/ Waterfield 1973, no. 19, catalogue p. 62, reproduced in color p. 63.

V & A/Snowman 1977, no. L11, catalogue p. 74.

REFERENCES

Snowman 1953, no. 262, reproduced.

Snowman 1962/64, p. 147, reproduced in color Plate XXIX.

Great Private Collections/Snowman, p. 243, reproduced in color p. 242.

Metropolitan Bulletin/McNab Dennis, p. 234, reproduced no. 8.

"Every One a Gem," *New York Sunday News,* January 19, 1969, p. 22, reproduced in color.

Villager/Sears p. 5.

Gregory Jensen, United Press International (review of the V & A/Snowman Fabergé Exhibition), July 8, 1977, syndicated.

57. *SILVER PRESENTATION PADDLE STEAMER*

29 in./740 mm.

MARKS: *HW, 88 kokoshnik alpha, FABERGÉ* on main deck aft; *HW, 88* on top deck aft. (Wigström).

ACC. NO. FAB76021

The silver model is made with two tiers of cabins, with further skylights to those on top. All the windows have panes of colored glass which can be lit from inside. Miniature silver tables and stools are placed on the upper deck; life boats, life belts and other equipment are in other relevant parts of the ship. The blued steel funnel has gilt ornaments and the interiors of the air ducts are enamelled. An arched panel above the paddle wheel is inscribed in Cyrillic: *For the Heir Czarevitch, Alexis Nicolaevitch from the Volga Shipbuilders* on a blue enamel band, the center of the plaque is gilt with the Imperial Eagle and date 1913. Pennants with the Imperial initials in scarlet on a white enamel ground fly from bow and stern. The interior has a musical movement which plays the airs: *God Save the Czar* and *Sailing Down the Volga.*

PROVENANCE

Presented to the Czarevitch Alexis by the Volga Shipbuilders, 1913.

Hammer Galleries, New York.

Charles Ward, President of Brown and Bigelow.

Franklin D. Roosevelt, "Top Cottage," Hyde Park, New York. Gift of Ward.

Elliott Roosevelt, New York, his son.

Wally Findlay.

Brandeis University (Sale: Sotheby Parke Bernet, New York, May 20, 1976, Lot 262 reproduced with glazed case, reproduced in color, Plate VIII).

EXHIBITION

"A Century of Progress," Marshall Field and Co., Chicago, 1933-34.

REFERENCES

Snowman 1953/55, p. 149, reproduced no. 254.

Snowman 1962/64, p. 164-5, reproduced no. 284.

Art at Auction/1975-76, New York and London, 1976, p. 259, reproduced in color.

Du/von Hapsburg, p. 87, reproduced.

57. *Silver Paddle Steamer (reduced 50%)*

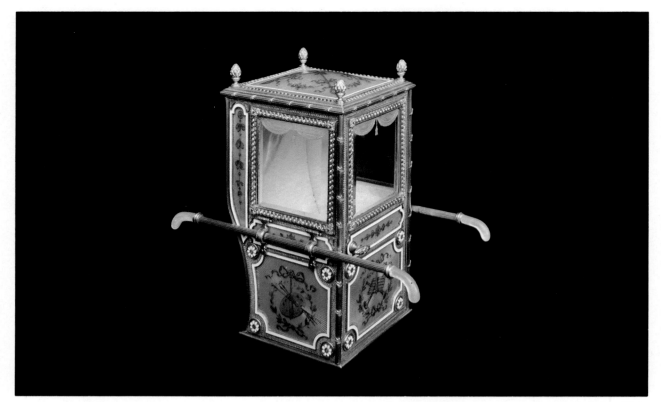

58. Sedan Chair

58. SEDAN CHAIR

3-1/2 in./85 mm.
MARKS: *FABERGÉ, 72 kokoshnik JL, MP* on base; *72* on
door edge. (Perchin).
CASE: Fitted black suede; 7-1/2 in./90 mm.; stamped in gold
A La Vieille Russie/781 Fifth Ave./New York.
ACC. NO. FAB66007

This miniature sedan chair in the Louis XVI taste is
made of gold enamelled a translucent salmon pink
painted in brown on the sides with a basket of
flowers and palette with brushes, the back with an
urn of flowers within formal scrolls and an amatory
trophy, the top with floral swags between crossed
batons, and the front with a musical trophy, each
within borders of opaque white enamel or green
ribbons about white pellets. It is lined with mother of
pearl, the crystal windows are engraved with curtains
and tassels. The two reeded gold carrying rods with
mother of pearl handles are detachable, held by two
hinged, pinned straps. The door opens by turning the
handle.

(See Appendix D for detail of rods).

An almost identical sedan chair was sold at Christie's,
Geneva on April 28, 1978, Lot 382. The differences
between the two and a color plate of the second
version appear in the catalogue, pp. 140-41.

PROVENANCE
J. P. Morgan, New York (Sale: Parke-Bernet, January 6, 7
and 8, 1944, Lot 430, catalogue p. 83, reproduced,
$1800.00).
Mr. and Mrs. Jack Linsky, New York.

A La Vieille Russie, New York.
Lansdell K. Christie, Long Island.
EXHIBITIONS
"Peter Carl Fabergé/Goldsmith and Jeweller to the Russian
Imperial Court," A La Vieille Russie, New York, No-
vember-December 1949, no. 183, catalogue.
"Loan Exhibition of the Art of Peter Carl Fabergé, Imperial
Court Jeweler," Hammer Galleries, New York, March
28-April 28, 1951, no. 293, catalogue p. 42, reproduced,
p. 43.
Corcoran 1961, no. 9, p. 31, reproduced in color p. 31.
ALVR 1961, no. 269, reproduced p. 56.
Metropolitan 1962-66, no. L.62.8.9.
ALVR 1968, no. 357, p. 134, reproduced in color p. 135.
NYCC/Waterfield 1973, no. 20, p. 11, 64, reproduced in
color p. 65.
V & A/Snowman 1977, no. L14, p. 74.
REFERENCES
Snowman 1953, no. 519, reproduced.
Snowman 1962/64, Plate L, reproduced in color.
Metropolitan Bulletin/McNab Dennis, p. 234-5, no. 10
reproduced p. 235.
FORBES, March 15, 1969, reproduced in color p. 72.
Esquire, reproduced in color p. 139.
Newsweek/Douglas, p. 85, reproduced in color p. 84.
Nineteenth Century/Snowman, reproduced p. 50.
Vogue Italia/Clay, reproduced in color p. 30.
Palm Beach Life/Watts, reproduced in color p. 38.
"Important Russian Works of Art," Christie's, Geneva,
April 28, 1978, catalogue p. 141.

59. GUERIDON

2-7/8 in./73 mm. top.
2-1/4 in./56 mm. high.
MARKS: *ET, ET, 56 St. George, KF* on leg.
ACC. NO. FAB69001

The Gueridon is made of gold with a circular crystal top, the center of which is inlaid with opals in blues and greens with fiery iridescence. The crystal is inset and applied with nine trails of green gold foliage. The legs are festooned with green-gold foliage with red-gold ribbons and ties.

PROVENANCE
Anon. Sale: Sotheby & Co., London, December 12, 1966, Lot 157, catalogue p. 45, reproduced.
A La Vieille Russie, New York.
EXHIBITIONS
ALVR 1968, No. 326, p. 137, reproduced.
NYCC/Waterfield 1973, no. 21, p. 66, reproduced in color p. 67.
REFERENCE
FORBES, April 15, 1970, p. 62, reproduced in color.

60. *BASKET OF LILIES OF THE VALLEY*

3-1/8 in./80 mm.
MARKS: *MP, 56* anchors, *FABERGÉ* on basket.
CASE: Fitted black morocco; 4-3/8 in./110 mm.; lining stamped in gold *A La Vieille Russie/785 Fifth Ave./New York.*
ACC. NO. FAB66012

Twenty-four exquisite sprays of lily-of-the-valley, each with finely engraved nephrite leaf; the flowers of pearls pierced by a fine gold thread and on gold stems, within finely woven gold basket filled with green gold worked as moss.

This piece is similar to the larger basket of lilies-of-the-valley in the collection of the Mathilda Geddings Gray Foundation in New Orleans.

PROVENANCE
Princess Marina, Dowager Duchess of Kent (Sale: Sotheby & Co., London, 1960. Princess Marina was the daughter of Grand Duke Vladimir, brother of Czar Alexander III).
Lansdell K. Christie, Long Island.
EXHIBITIONS
Corcoran 1961, no. 11, p. 54, reproduced in color p. 53.
Metropolitan 1962-66, no. L.62.8.90.
NYCC/Waterfield 1973, no. 18, catalogue p. 62, reproduced in color p. 63 and on front cover.
V & A/Snowman 1977, no. L10, catalogue pp. 73-74, reproduced in color p. 82.
REFERENCES
Sotheby's 206th Season, London, 1960, p. 67, reproduced.
Snowman 1962/64, Plate LXV, reproduced in color.
Great Private Collections/Snowman, p. 243, reproduced in color p. 242.
FORBES, August 15, 1969, p. 54, reproduced in color.
A. K. Snowman, "Carl Fabergé—Decorator Extraordinary," *The Society of Silver Collectors*, December 1970, p. 88.
Newsweek/Douglas, p. 85, reproduced in color p. 84.
Villager/Sears, p. 5.
Kate Dyson, "Fabergé Show Intrigues London Crowds," *Antique Monthly*, August 1977, p. 13A, reproduced in color.
Jean Nichols, "The Arts . . . and You," *News-Virginian*, Waynesboro, April 19, 1978.

59. Gueridon

60. Basket of Lilies

BOXES

The tradition of elaborate presentation boxes as symbols of Royal or Imperial favor or rewards for services to the throne was a long established one. In an era of unparalleled ostentation, Fabergé's presentation boxes are noteworthy for their restraint and relative simplicity of design. The Coronation Box presented by Czarina Alexandra Feodorovna to Nicholas II, in 1897, is the firm's masterpiece of the genre. In addition to purely decorative presentation boxes, the growing popularity of cigarette smoking and pill taking created new excuses for beautiful boxes, as had the vogue for snuff during an earlier period. Fabergé's boxes for these and other purposes are often virtuoso performances of the art, but, more so than in other areas, derivative of the works of earlier jewellers and goldsmiths.

61. Coronation Box

61. CORONATION BOX

3-3/4 in./95 mm.
MARKS: *FABERGÉ, AH, 56 anchors* inside lid; *AH* inside
lid rim; *FABERGÉ, AH, 56 anchors* inside base;
anchors inside base rim; scratched *1067*.
CASE: Fitted green morocco, lid applied with gilt-metal
Imperial Eagle; 5-1/4 in./133 mm.; lid lining unstamped.
ACC. NO. FAB66009

The gold box is enamelled a translucent yellow, the
base and sides over an engine-turned ground, the
cover over sunbursts which are defined by a chased
gold trelliswork set with diamonds at the intersections. At the center of each sunburst is a double-
headed Imperial Eagle in black enamel with a
diamond set at the center of the body. At the center
of the box itself is applied a cypher of Nicholas II in
rose diamonds on a translucent white enamel panel
within a border of diamonds with a crown above.

The eagles are fixed by pins into the cover of the box.
These holes had to be drilled underwater so as not to
heat and so disfigure the enamel which had already
been applied to the surface of the box. The Coronation Egg is decorated in the same manner.

PROVENANCE
Presented by Czarina Alexandra Feodorovna to her hus-
band, Nicholas II, 1897.
Herr Bomm, Vienna (an emigré Russian journalist, sold
1938).
Sidney Hill, London and New York.
Wartski, London.
Arthur E. Bradshaw.
Lansdell K. Christie, Long Island.
EXHIBITIONS
Corcoran 1961, no. 14, catalogue p. 33, reproduced in
color p. 4.
ALVR 1961, no. 93, catalogue p. 43, reproduced in color
p. 49.
Metropolitan 1962-66, no. L.62.8.14.
NYCC/Waterfield 1973, p. 52, reproduced in color p. 53.
V & A/Snowman 1977, no. 014, catalogue pp. 98-99,
reproduced in color p. 81.
REFERENCES
Henry and Sidney Hill, *Antique Gold Boxes*, New York,
1953, p. 194, reproduced no. 204.
Snowman 1962/64, Plate I, reproduced in color.
Great Private Collections/Snowman, p. 244, reproduced in
color p. 245.
FORBES, October 15, 1969, p. 54.
"Splendors of the Court," *The Horizon Book of the Arts of
Russia*, New York, 1970, p. 168, reproduced.
A. K. Snowman, "Carl Fabergé—Decorator Extraor-
dinary," *The Society of Silver Collectors*, London, Decem-
ber 1970, p. 87.
Esquire, p. 139, reproduced in color.
Nineteenth Century/Snowman, p. 51, reproduced.
Vogue Italia/Clay, p. 129, reproduced in color.
Jean Nichols, "The Arts . . . and You," *News-Virginian*,
Waynesboro, April 19, 1978.

62. BLUE ROCAILLE BOX

3-3/4 in./95 mm.
MARKS: *MP, 56 anchors* inside lid; *anchors* inside lid rim;
MP, 56 anchors inside base; *MP, anchors, FABERGÉ*
outside base rim; scratched *1111*.
ACC. NO. FAB78005

Enamelled translucent royal blue over an engraved
gold starburst ground, the box is applied with
elaborately chased diamond-set gold scroll work in
the rococo style. To the left is the crowned cypher of
Czar Nicholas II set with rose diamonds on a
translucent white enamel oval bordered with
diamonds. One of these conceals the release which
when triggered causes the cypher to rise on a hinge
concealed in the crown to reveal a miniature of the
Czar. The sides and bottom of the box are framed
with reeded gold bands and also enamelled royal blue
on less flamboyantly engraved gold grounds.

An almost identically decorated surprise presentation
box with a nephrite top and green enamelled sides
was sold at Christie's in Geneva on April 26, 1978,
Lot 380 and is reproduced in color in the catalogue.

PROVENANCE
Czar Nicholas II, presented to an unidentified personage,
1895-1903.
A La Vieille Russie, New York.
EXHIBITION
ALVR 1968, no. 304, catalogue p. 116, reproduced.
REFERENCES
"The Gold of All the Russias," *Apollo*, November 1968, pp.
392, 394, reproduced open and closed figs. 3, 4.
"Important Russian Works of Art," Christie's, Geneva,
April 26, 1978, p. 138.

63. NICHOLAS II NEPHRITE BOX

3-3/4 in./95 mm.
MARKS: *kokoshnik, HW, 56* on lid rim; *kokoshnik, HW, 56,
FABERGÉ* on base rim; scratched *4909*. (Wigström).
CASE: Original fitted hollywood; 7-1/8 in./181 mm.; lid
lining stamped in black, *Eagle/FABERGÉ/Petrograd/
Moscow London*.
ACC. NO. FAB66021

The box is hollowed from two pieces of nephrite, the
cover applied with a rose diamond trellis about a
wreath of laurel foliage enclosing a portrait by Zuiev
of Nicholas II wearing the uniform of the 4th
(Imperial Family) Rifle Battalion of Guards and the
Cross of the Order of St. George. The mounts are of
gold, those to the rim chased in green gold with
foliage.

Nicholas II was awarded the Cross of St. George in
1915.

PROVENANCE
Czar Nicholas II presented to an unidentified personage,
1915-16.
Mrs. J. M. Jacques, England.
Lansdell K. Christie, Long Island.

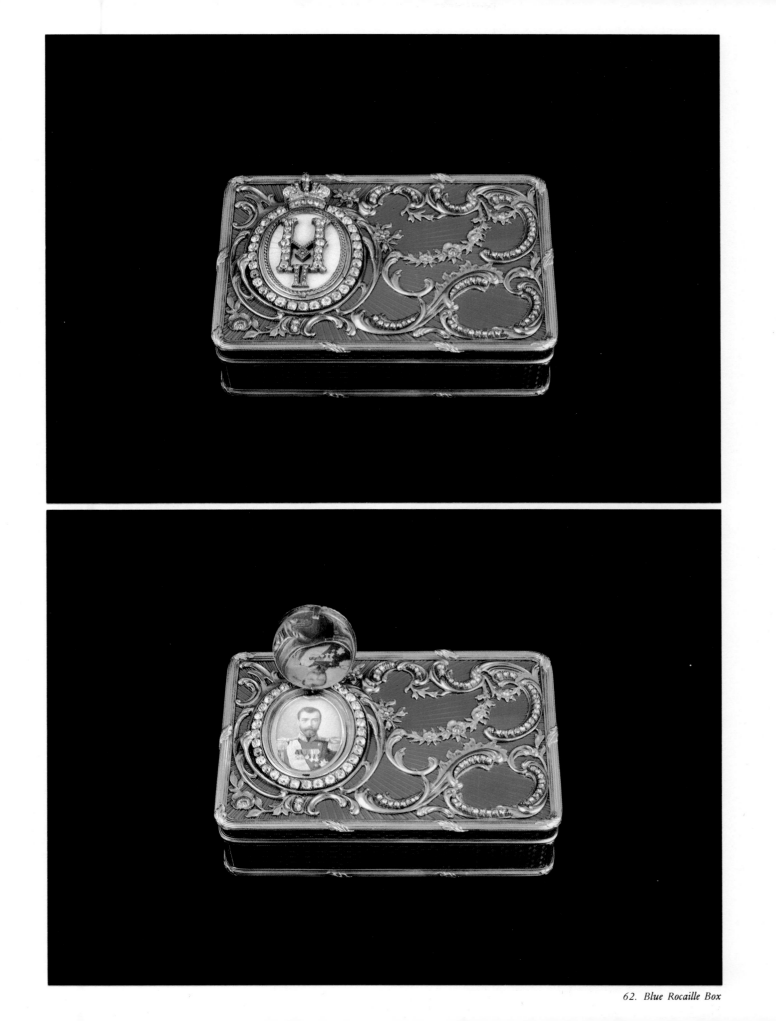

62. Blue Rocaille Box

EXHIBITIONS

"A Loan Exhibition of the Works of Carl Fabergé,"
Wartski, London, November 8-25, 1949, no. 259,
catalogue p. 251.

"Special Coronation Exhibition of the Work of Carl
Fabergé," Wartski, London, May 20-June 15, 1953, no.
158, catalogue p. 16.

Metropolitan 1962-66, no. L.62.8.156.

NYCC/Waterfield 1973, no. 13, catalogue p. 54, reproduced in color p. 55.

V & A/Snowman 1977, no. L9, catalogue p. 73.

REFERENCES

Bainbridge 1949/66, Plate 125(b), reproduced.

Snowman 1953, no. 122, reproduced.

Snowman 1962/64, no. 130, reproduced.

Metropolitan Bulletin/McNab Dennis, p. 240, reproduced
no. 21.

FORBES, July 1, 1969, p. 51, reproduced in color.

A.K. Snowman, "Carl Fabergé-Decorator Extraordinary,"
Society of Silver Collectors, December 1970, p. 86, reproduced.

Esquire, p. 139, reproduced in color.

Vogue Italia/Clay, p. 129, reproduced in color.

64. GOLD PRESENTATION CIGARETTE CASE

3-3/4 in./95 mm.

MARKS: *GN, kokoshnik* inside lid; *GN, 56 kokoshnik, JL,*
inside base; *ET, ET,* on lid edge. (Niukkanen).

The collection of Mrs. Malcolm S. Forbes

The plain polished gold case is applied at one corner
with the Imperial Eagle set with rose diamonds and a
single brilliant. The thumbpiece is set with a
cabochon sapphire.

Similar cigarette cases were presented on many
occasions to those who had faithfully served members
of the Imperial Family. This was the first piece of
Fabergé acquired by Malcolm S. Forbes.

PROVENANCE

Bentley & Co., London.

EXHIBITION

NYCC/Waterfield 1973, no. 14, catalogue pp. 3, 56,
reproduced in color p. 57.

REFERENCES

FORBES, August 15, 1972, p. 72, reproduced in color.

Home News/Cook p. C1-2.

Vogue Italia/Clay, p. 129, reproduced in color.

"Important Russian Works of Art" Christie's, Geneva,
April 26, 1978, p. 106.

65. LOUIS XVI SNUFFBOX, Blerzy

3-1/4 in./82 mm.

MARKS: Joseph Etienne Blerzy, date letter O for 1777,
Paris, charge and decharge of J. B. Fouache, farmer-
general from 1774-80, inside lid; each repeated inside
bottom.

CASE: Fitted gray morocco; 4-3/4 in./120 mm.; stamped in
gold on lid liner *Crest/by Appointment to/H. M. The
Queen/Jewellers/WARTSKI/138 Regent St./London &
Llandudno.*

ACC. NO. FAB66019

The gold oval box is red enamelled with panels
enclosed by borders of berried foliage and white trails
of pellets with additional simulated enamel rubies on
the cover. The center of the cover is set with a plaque
painted with a scene from classical history.

This box is one of the most popular types of snuff-
boxes made at the end of the reign of Louis XV and
during the reign of Louis XVI, and by one of the most
prolific makers of this shape, the other two being Le
Bastier and Barrière.

PROVENANCE

Czarina Catherine II, The Hermitage.

Czar Paul I, her son.

Czar Alexander I, his son.

Czar Nicholas I, his brother.

Czar Alexander II, his son.

Czar Alexander III, his son.

Czar Nicholas II, his son.

Wartski, London.

Lansdell K. Christie, Long Island.

EXHIBITIONS

Corcoran 1961, no. 15, catalogue p. 33.

Metropolitan 1962-66, no. L.62.8.15.

ALVR 1968, no. 320, catalogue p. 122, reproduced.

NYCC/Waterfield 1973, no. 16, catalogue p. 11, 60,
reproduced in color p. 61.

V & A/Snowman 1977, no. L16, catalogue p. 75.

REFERENCES

Snowman 1953, no. 43, reproduced.

Snowman 1962/64, no. 52, reproduced.

FORBES, February 15, 1970, p. 46, reproduced in color.

A. K. Snowman, "Carl Fabergé—Decorator Extraordinary," The Society of Silver Collectors, London, December 1970, p. 86.

Vogue Italia/Clay, p. 130, reproduced in color.

66. LOUIS XVI-STYLE SNUFFBOX

3-1/4 in./82 mm.

MARKS: *FABERGÉ, 72 anchors, MP* inside base;
scratched *7690.* (Perchin).

CASE: Fitted gray morocco; 4-3/4 in./120 mm.; stamped in
gold on lid lining *Crest/by Appointment to/H. M. The
Queen/Jewellers/WARTSKI/138 Regent St./London &
Llandudno.*

ACC. NO. FAB66020

The gold box is enamelled green and the panels are
enclosed by formal foliage and the cover embellished
with simulated opals, the plaque on the cover is 18th
century and enamelled with Venus and Cupid, set
within a border of rose diamonds.

The French box above is reputed to have been in the
Imperial Collection at the Hermitage. Alexander III is
said to have challenged Fabergé to match the skill of
the eighteenth-century goldsmiths. He was so im-
pressed with the Russian version that he ordered
them both to be placed on view in the public galleries
of the Winter Palace.

PROVENANCE

Czar Alexander III, The Hermitage.

Czar Nicholas II, his son.

63. Nicholas II Nephrite Box

64. Gold Cigarette Case

65. Louis XVI Snuffbox, Blerzy

66. Louis XVI-Style Snuffbox

Wartski, London.
Lansdell K. Christie, Long Island.

EXHIBITIONS
Corcoran 1961, no. 16, catalogue p. 33, reproduced in color p. 39.
Metropolitan 1962-66, no. L.62.8.16.
ALVR 1968, no. 321, catalogue p. 122, reproduced.
NYCC/Waterfield 1973, no. 17, catalogue p. 11, 60, reproduced in color p. 61.
V & A/Snowman 1977, no. L17, catalogue p. 75.
REFERENCES
Snowman, 1953, Plate VI, reproduced in color.
Snowman, 1962/64, Plate IX, reproduced in color.
Great Private Collections/Snowman, p. 244, reproduced in color p. 245.
FORBES, February 15, 1970, p. 46, reproduced in color.
A. K. Snowman, "Carl Fabergé—Decorator Extraordinary," *The Society of Silver Collectors*, London, December 1970, p. 86.
Vogue Italia/Clay, p. 130, reproduced in color.

67. Circular Bonbonnière (reduced 8%)

67. CIRCULAR BONBONNIÈRE

1-5/8 in./42 mm.
MARKS: *56 anchors, MP, FABERGÉ* on lower rim; scratched *47020* (Perchin).
ACC. NO. FAB 76027

The base and hinged cover of this circular gold box are set eccentrically with circular panels of crystal engraved with a heart on crossed arrows and laurel, respectively. The sides and border to the cover are set with rose diamonds in star-like collets on alternating curved panels of blue enamel and matted gold engraved with fine foliage. The base is decorated with the curved panels but without the diamonds. The thumbpiece is in the form of a rose diamond-set scallop shell.

PROVENANCE
Ortman-Blickman, New York.

68. VINAIGRETTE

7/8 in./21 mm.
MARKS: *kokoshnik IL, KF* inside lid; *KF, 56 kokoshnik IL* inside base; scratched *8478*.
CASE: Original fitted hollywood; 2 in./45 mm.; lid lining stamped in gold, *Eagle/K. FABERGÉ/Moscow/S. Petersburg Odessa*.
ACC. NO. FAB 76023

This tiny gold box of octagonal form is enamelled a turquoise blue, the base and cover painted in dark green with entwined foliage and a pineapple rod resembling a caduceus; with rose diamond-set thumbpiece.

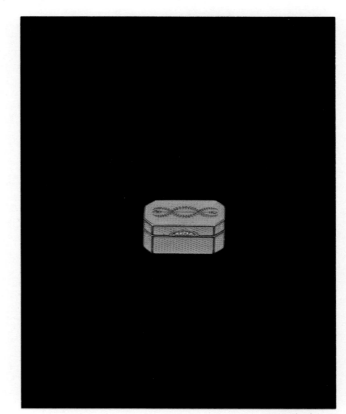

68. Vinaigrette

PROVENANCE
Anon. Sale: Sotheby & Co., London, February 18, 1974, Lot 152, catalogue p. 31, reproduced Plate VI.
Ortman-Blickman, New York.
REFERENCE
Ian Bennet, *Antiques £10—£1000*, London 1974, p. 59.

FRAMES

The proliferation of photography during the last decades of the nineteenth century created an enormous market for frames. Miniatures had always been popular souvenirs among the rich and powerful. Photography only made it easier to indulge this passion for visual evidence of the affection of one's family or the acquaintance of important personages. The House of Fabergé catered to this demand with its usual imagination, brilliant selection of materials and unsurpassed craftsmanship. Among the frames illustrated herein is the largest and most spectacular example created for the Imperial Family, a delightful surprise frame commemorating the birth of Grand Duchess Tatiana and a superb double-sided frame in the form of a fire-screen.

69. Imperial Presentation Frame (reduced 36%)

69. IMPERIAL PRESENTATION FRAME

14-5/8 in./372 mm.
MARKS: *FABERGÉ, 56 kokoshnik JL, MP* on edge; *88* strut top; *MP, JL kokoshnik 88* strut back. (Perchin).

CASE: Original fitted hollywood, lid applied with white metal Imperial Crown; 19 in./480 mm.; lid lining stamped: *Eagle / K. FABERGÉ / St. Petersburg / Moscow.* Zippered pale green velvet slip-cover.
ACC. NO. FAB65003

The frame is of gold set with rock crystal panels engraved with foliage, the mounts are chased in high relief with laurel foliage enamelled green with white ties, the square corner panels and six roundels in the border are enamelled salmon pink and applied with motifs in four colors of gold and rose diamonds. The motifs at the corners are the Imperial Crown, that above is the cipher of Maria Feodorovna, that below the Imperial Eagle, the sides have musical, gardening and amatory trophies. At the back is a silver-gilt scroll strut applied with an Imperial Crown. The frame contains a period print of a photograph of Czar Nicholas II wearing the uniform of the Life Guard Hussars (His Majesty's Regiment).

(Appendix D for detail of strut).

PROVENANCE
Presented by Czar Alexander III to his wife, Maria Feodorovna.
Maurice Sandoz, Switzerland.
A La Vieille Russie, New York.
EXHIBITIONS
ALVR 1968, no. 322, p. 112, reproduced in color p. 123.
NYCC/Waterfield 1973, no. 26, p. 74, reproduced in color p. 75.
V & A/Snowman 1977, no. L3, p. 71.
REFERENCES
FORBES, March 15, 1968, p. 74, reproduced in color.
Nineteenth Century/Snowman, p. 53 reproduced in color.
Du/von Hapsburg, 57, reproduced.

70. HEART SURPRISE FRAME

3-1/4 in./82 mm. closed.
2-7/8 in./75 mm. open.
MARKS: inscribed in script *K Fabergé* on base.
ACC. NO. FAB78004

A scarlet-enamelled, engraved gold heart set with the date 1897 in rose diamonds and similarly bordered, springs open when the faceted shaft is depressed to reveal a dazzling green-enamelled shamrock, the leaves of which are set with diamond-bordered miniatures of Czar Nicholas II in uniform, his wife Alexandra and their second daughter Tatiana, whose birth in 1897 this piece commemorates. The hexagonal tapering stem is enamelled opaque white and painted with spiraling garlands of green foliage. Bands of gold, alternately decorated with scarlet enamel, or chased geometrically, or set with diamonds encircle the tiered base ending before the stem in a band of chased gold palm leaves. One of the four pearls set on the laurel-wreathed, scarlet-enamelled central band of the base conceals a release —a slight touch and the miniatures disappear, transformed once again into a heart.

A similar frame in the Louis XV style with a stand and shaft of chased gold and a pink enamel heart is the surprise of the Rocaille Egg presented by Alexander Ferdinandovitch Kelch to his wife in 1902. The original miniatures in this later frame, as with those in the Kelch Hen Egg (Catalogue no. 10), have had others substituted for them.

(Appendix D for detail of inscription).

PROVENANCE
Lady Lydia Deterding, Paris (Sale: Christie's, Geneva, April 26, 1978, Lot 381, catalogue p. 138, reproduced in color open and closed, Plate 49).
REFERENCE
Snowman 1964, no. 103, reproduced.

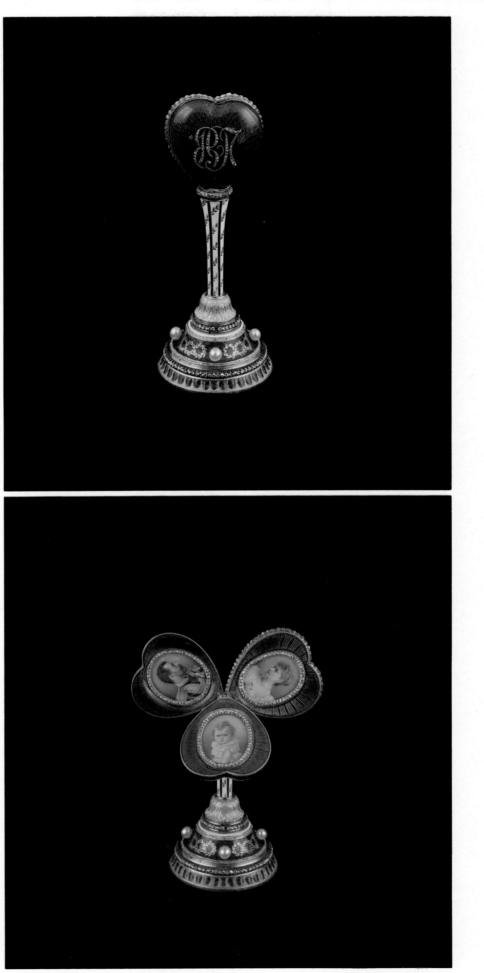

70. Heart Surprise Frame

71. FIRE-SCREEN FRAME

7-1/8 in./180 mm.

MARKS: *HW, alpha kokoshnik 72, kokoshnik, FABERGÉ* on bottom edge. (Wigström).

CASE: Original fitted hollywood; 8 in./125 mm.; lid lining stamped in black, *Eagle/FABERGÉ/Petrograd/Moscow Odessa.*

ACC. NO. FAB73005

The rectangular gold panel is enamelled on one side a translucent white, the other a translucent pink, and each side is almost entirely covered by the husk wreath and swags of flowers chased in four-color gold, held by red gold knots of ribbon. On either side are cylindrical pillars of banded white enamel entwined with a spiral of vari-colored gold flowers and with pearl finials.

The cresting is formed by four sprays of laurel about a bracket which holds the vari-colored gold wreath in the center.

A line of white enamel guilloche ornament runs above and below the enamelled panel; the oval apertures have pearl borders within narrow white enamel bands. A pineapple suspended from acanthus fronds is chased in green gold between the four scroll supports which are chased with further acanthus ornament, the whole resting on four reeded stud feet. The photographs are of Nicholas II and Alexandra Feodorovna.

This frame may be considered a perfect example of conventional Edwardian taste. There was a constant demand for the formal sweetness of such a design by those who eschewed Art Nouveau and Art Deco.

PROVENANCE
Maurice Sandoz, Switzerland.
Lansdell K. Christie, Long Island.
A La Vieille Russie, New York.

EXHIBITIONS
ALVR 1961, no. 183, p. 63, reproduced p. 68.
Corcoran 1961, no. 6, pp. 18, 26, reproduced in color (both sides) p. 27.
Metropolitan 1962-66, no. L62.8.6.
ALVR 1968, no. 365, p. 137, reproduced in color.
V & A/Snowman 1977, no. L1, p. 71.

REFERENCES
Snowman 1962/64, p. 147, reproduced in color Plate XXVII.
"Every one a gem," *New York Sunday News,* January 19, 1969, p. 23 reproduced in color.
FORBES, March 15, 1974, p. 69, reproduced in color (both sides).
N.Y. Times/Reif, p. C17.

71. Fire screen frame (recto)

(verso)

72. CRYSTAL FRAME

4 in./102 mm.
MARKS: *56 JL, MP* on strut; scratched *5956.* (Perchin).
ACC. NO. FAB74006

The shaped-rectangular rock crystal frame is etched with a band of notched ornament and applied with festoons of flowers chased in four colors of gold. The finial is in the form of a basket of flowers also chased in vari-colored gold and set with rose diamonds and cabochon rubies; pink enamel ribbons float to each side. Below a pink bow centered by a cabochon ruby suspends a rose diamond tassel, and the two stud feet are also set with rose diamonds. With rose diamond border to the aperture which contains a modern print of a photograph of the Grand Duchess Marie. On the back is an ivory panel hinged with the gold scroll strut.

(Appendix D for detail of strut).

PROVENANCE
A La Vieille Russie, New York.
EXHIBITION
"Peter Carl Fabergé/Goldsmith and Jeweller to the Russian Imperial Court," A La Vieille Russie, New York, November-December 1949, no. 179, catalogue, reproduced.
REFERENCE
FORBES, August 15, 1975, p. 58, reproduced in color.

73. LATTICE-WORK FRAME

4-1/4 in./115 mm.
MARKS: *BA, 56 anchors, FABERGÉ* on back; *BA, 56 anchors* on strut; scratched *58804.* (Aarne).
ACC. NO. FAB73002

The gold frame is formed by four reeded rods entwined with chased green gold foliage, the flame finials are enamelled scarlet and there are white ties where they overlap. The rods enclose a trellis with quatrefoil pearl clusters through which is looped a floral wreath chased in four colors of gold, which forms a surround for the oval pearl-bordered aperture. With laurel wreath and ribbon tie cresting, and a gold strut. The frame now contains a modern print of a photograph of Czar Nicholas II in uniform.

(Appendix D for detail of strut).

PROVENANCE
A La Vieille Russie, New York.
REFERENCE
FORBES, September 15, 1973, p. 115, reproduced in color.

72. Crystal Frame

73. Lattice-Work Frame

74. *MARIE PAVLOVNA MIRROR*

8-7/8 in./226 mm.
MARKS: *FABERGÉ, BA, 88 kokoshnik JL*, on bottom edge,
   scratched *90017, UIM/-/-.* (Aarne).
ACC. NO. FAB77002

The frame is of silver-gilt enamelled a translucent scarlet and chased with seven Imperial Eagles. At the top is the crowned monogram of Grand Duchess Marie Pavlovna in rose diamonds on a circular white enamel panel; there is a corded border to the rectangular aperture which contains a mirror, and the outer border is chased with egg and lozenge motif.

The monogram is that of the Grand Duchess Marie Pavlovna (1854-1920), Duchess of Mecklenburg, who married the Grand Duke Vladimir Alexandrovitch, brother of Alexander III, in 1874.

(Appendix D for detail of strut).

PROVENANCE
Grand Duchess Marie Pavlovna.
Anon. Sale: Sotheby's Belgravia, London, April 7, 1977,
   Lot 49, catalogue p. 14, reproduced in color.
Wartski, London.

75. *PALE BLUE FRAME*

8-1/4 in./210 mm.
MARKS: *FABERGÉ, 91 kokoshnik AP, AN* on border;
   FABERGÉ, AN, AP kokoshnik 91 on bottom edge;
   scratched *15788.* (Nevalainen).
ACC. NO. FAB76031

The silver-gilt frame has a panel of pale blue translucent enamel with applied rosettes at the corners, chased laurel swags and pendants above descend from the knot of ribbon cresting. With chased palmette border to the rectangular aperture, outer reed and tie border. With silver-gilt strut and hollywood back. It now contains a postcard portrait of the Czarevitch in a sailor suit with the name of the Imperial yacht 'Standart' on his cap-band. The card was sent by Czarina Alexandra Feodorovna to her Lady-in-Waiting, Princess Marie Bariatinsky. It is written in English and reads:

   To Dearest Clary,
   With heartiest X-mas wishes & blessings for the
   coming year 1909.
   fr. yr. very loving,
   Alexandra

74. *Marie Pavlovna Mirror (reduced 17%)*

75. *Pale Blue Frame*

The hollywood back has been temporarily replaced with plexiglass in order that this message may be seen.

The center pendant is a replacement.

(Appendix D for detail of strut).

PROVENANCE
Anon. Sale: Sotheby Parke Bernet, New York, December 10, 1976, Lot 415, reproduced in catalogue.
A La Vieille Russie, New York.

76. *AMATORY FRAME*

4-1/8 in./105 mm.
MARKS: *FABERGÉ, 56 anchors, MP* on bottom edge; scratched *45847, 288N IM/-/-*. (Perchin).
ACC. NO. FAB76001

The rectangular panel is enamelled a translucent pink within a gold mount chased with egg and dart motif. It has an oval aperture above which is festooned swags of flowers chased in four colors of gold upon which are perched two doves. The red gold ribbon cresting suspends a musical trophy which falls between the doves.

Below the oval are chased green gold sprays of laurel, and within a geometric motif stand two putti holding palms with musical and amatory trophies about them. With gold strut to the ivory back. The frame now contains a modern print of a photograph of Czarina Maria Feodorovna and her sister Queen Alexandra of Britain.

(Appendix D for detail of strut).

PROVENANCE
Anon. Sale: Sotheby's Belgravia, London, November 6, 1975, Lot 68, catalogue p. 20, reproduced with original photograph.
A La Vieille Russie, New York.
REFERENCE
FORBES, February 6, 1978, p. 77, reproduced in color.

76. Amatory Frame

77. PINK OVAL FRAME

3 in./75 mm.
MARKS: *MP, 56 kokoshnik* on side edge; scratched *2640, UI/-/-.(Perchin)*.
ACC. NO. FAB76002

The oval translucent pink panel has gold mounts, those to the outer border chased in green gold with a guilloche pattern, the inner border with laurel foliage and further inner border of reeded red gold: gold strut to the ivory back.

The miniature is of an unidentified lady in a costume of the 1780's.

(Appendix D for detail of strut).

PROVENANCE
Anon. Sale: Sotheby's Belgravia, London, November 6, 1975, Lot 69, catalogue p. 20, reproduced.
A La Vieille Russie, New York.

78. WHITE FRAME

2-3/4 in./70 mm.
MARKS: *FABERGÉ, MP, 56 kokoshnik JL* on bottom edge, *FABERGÉ, MP, 56 kokoshnik, ET, ET* on strut; scratched *2759*. (Perchin).
ACC. NO. FAB76018

The rectangular gold panel is engraved as a sunburst and enamelled a translucent white within a border of green gold laurel foliage with red gold rosettes at the angles. The oval aperture is chased with laurel foliage enamelled green and set with rose diamond ties. With a gold strut to the ivory back. The frame now contains a modern print of a photograph of Czarevitch Alexis in uniform.

(Appendix D for detail of strut).

PROVENANCE
Anon. Sale: Christie's, Geneva, April 28, 1976, Lot 199, catalogue p. 55, reproduced in color Plate 42.
Jan Skala, New York.

79. VIEUX-ROSE FRAME

2-7/8 in./75 mm.
MARKS: *JA, 56 kokoshnik AP, FABERGÉ* on bottom edge; *swan* on strut, scratched *14729*. (Armfelt).
ACC. NO. FAB76017

The square gold frame is enamelled a translucent *vieux rose* over a swag motif and has applied chased green gold laurel swags and pendants from three seed pearls, one forming the center of the red ribbon cresting. Two further pearls are set in the corners below. There are two gold stud feet and a gold scroll strut on the ivory back.

The frame now contains a modern print of a photograph of Czar Nicholas II in uniform.

(Appendix D for detail of strut).

PROVENANCE
Anon. Sale: Christie's, Geneva, April 28, 1976, Lot 197, catalogue p. 54, reproduced in color plate 42.
Jan Skala, New York.

80. LAUREL-SPRIG FRAME

4 in./102 mm.
MARKS: *MP, 56 anchors* on bottom edge; *MP, 56 anchors* on strut; *anchors* on loop; scratched *59691*. (Perchin).
ACC. NO. FAB75001

The rectangular pink enamel panel has four triangular panels of pale blue enamel on which are applied sprigs of laurel in chased green gold within narrow borders. Each panel is divided by a red gold rosette and there is a red gold knot of ribbon cresting. On two reeded stud feet; with simple bifurcated gold strut from a tortoiseshell back. The frame now contains a modern print of a photograph of Czar Nicholas II in yachting attire.

(Appendix D for detail of strut).

PROVENANCE
Juvel og Kunst, Copenhagen.

81. KAISER WILHELM II FRAME

11-3/4 in./298 mm.
MARKS: *Eagle FABERGÉ, AN, 91 kokoshnik AP* on bottom edge. (Nevalainen).
ACC. NO. FAB76008

The rectangular silver-gilt frame is enamelled a pale translucent blue and at each corner is applied a wreath of chased oak and laurel foliage held by knots of ribbon. The large oval aperture has a chased laurel border and encloses a portrait of Kaiser Wilhelm II of Germany, signed by him and dated 1909. With reed and tie outer border and hollywood panel reverse; the hollywood strut is carved from a further panel into which it fits.

77. Pink Oval Frame

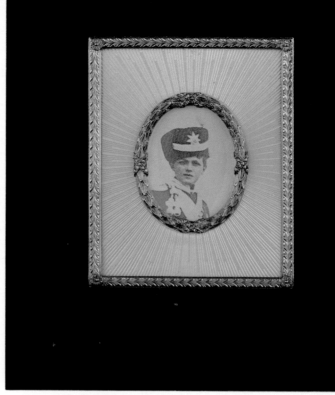

78. White Frame

79. Vieux-Rose Frame

80. Laurel-Sprig Frame

81. *Kaiser Wilhelm II Frame (reduced 27%)*

82. Double Agate Frame

The portrait and frame were obviously intended for an important Briton, possibly one of the Kaiser's many Royal English cousins. Not only is the photograph signed *William. Feb. 1909, Berlin* (i.e. in English and not in German), but the higher standard of silver (91 not 88 or 84) was demanded by the English Assay Office.

(Appendix D for detail of strut).

PROVENANCE
Presented by Kaiser Wilhelm II to an unknown personage, Berlin, February 1909.
Juvel og Kunst, Copenhagen.

82. DOUBLE AGATE FRAME

6-1/4 in./158 mm.
8 in./204 mm. open.

MARKS: *Eagle FABERGÉ, AN, 88 kokoshnik JL* on bottom edge; *AN, 88 kokoshnik JL* on side edge; scratched *7259.* (Nevalainen).
ACC. NO. FAB75007

The silver-gilt frame encloses two arched rectangular panels of opaque, creamy, pinkish-brown agate, each with an oval aperture within reed and tie border beneath applied silver-gilt laurel swags and pendants suspended from three knots of ribbon. The borders are beaded and rest on three gadrooned stud feet, with three pineapple finials above, the central finial on the hinge. The back is enclosed by two wood panels.

PROVENANCE
Anon. Sale: Christie's, Geneva, November 11, 1975, Lot 249, catalogue p. 63, reproduced Plate 21.
A La Vieille Russie, New York.

83. *Carelian Birch Frame*

83. *CARELIAN BIRCH FRAME*

5-1/2 in./140 mm.
MARKS: *AN, 88 kokoshnik AP* on mounts; scratched *1912 Spala*. (Nevalainen).
ACC. NO. FAB76016

The arched rectangular panel of carelian birch has an applied foliage wreath in silver-gilt above the rectangular aperture, and a rosette in each corner. It contains the original photograph of the Czarevitch on board the Imperial yacht 'Standart'.

The strut is carved from a panel of carelian birch into which it fits. The Czarevitch wears a sailor's uniform with the name of the yacht on his cap-band.

(Appendix D for detail of strut).

PROVENANCE
Princess Henry of Prussia, née Princess Irene of Hesse, younger sister of Czarina Alexandra Feodorovna, née Princess Alix of Hesse.
Anon. Sale: Christie's, Geneva, April 28, 1976, Lot 171, catalogue p. 48, reproduced Plate 31.

Jan Skala, New York.
REFERENCE
FORBES, March 1, 1977, p. 81, reproduced in color.

84. *LARGE HOLLYWOOD FRAME*

13-1/4 in./337 mm.
MARKS: *FABERGÉ, 88 kokoshnik alpha, IP* on border. (Rappoport).
ACC. NO. FAB76007

The rectangular hollywood frame is inset with a silver-gilt panel enamelled a translucent blue within chased palmette borders. The hollywood strut is carved from the back panel into which it fits. The frame now contains a modern print of a photograph of Czar Nicholas II and Alexandra Feodorovna at a shoot.

(Appendix D for detail of strut).

PROVENANCE
Juvel og Kunst, Copenhagen.
REFERENCE
FORBES, March 1, 1977, p. 81, reproduced in color.

84. *Large Hollywood Frame (reduced 29%)*

OBJETS DE LUXE

Bagatelles for the bored and beautiful. The understated elegance of Fabergé's *objets de luxe* appealed to the rich and titled not only of Russia but of the world. For oriental potentates, European peers, American plutocrats and Russian autocrats something from Fabergé was very much a fashionable thing. Whatever the need—cuff links for the Czar's brother or knitting needles for a domestically-minded duchess, Fabergé always had the perfect little something.

85. *Ostrich-Feather Fan (reduced 66%)*

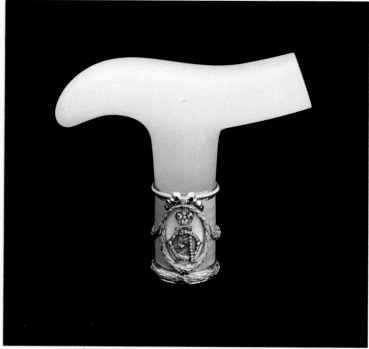

86. Imperial Parasol Handle

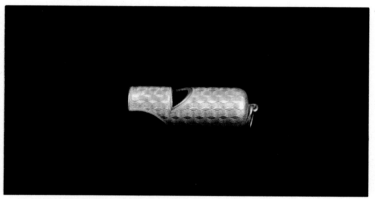

87. Pink Whistle

88. Pink Handle

85. OSTRICH-FEATHER FAN

20-1/2 in./530 mm.
HANDLE: 7 in./180 mm.
MARKS: *FABERGÉ, HW, 56* on loop; scratched *17349*. (Wigström).
CASE: Fitted burgundy morocco; 23 in./585 mm.; lining stamped in gold (twice), *crest/by Appointment/WARTSKI /LTD./138 Regent Street/London W 1/and Llandudno*.
ACC. NO. FAB69007

The six white ostrich feathers issue from the circular gold mount which is enamelled a translucent salmon-pink and applied with a rose diamond floral circlet, the reverse is set with a mirror, the rock crystal handle has similarly enamelled mounts and a ring from which are suspended silken tassels.

PROVENANCE
Peter Otway Smithers, M.P. (Sale: Sotheby's, London, December 8, 1969, Lot 83, catalogue p. 38, reproduced opposite).
EXHIBITIONS
"A Loan Exhibition of the Works of Carl Fabergé," Wartski, London, November 8-25, 1949, no. 229, catalogue p. 20.
"Special Coronation Exhibition of the Works of Carl Fabergé," Wartski, London, May 20-June 13, 1953, no. 19, catalogue p. 19.
NYCC/Waterfield 1973, no. 34, catalogue p. 84, reproduced in color p. 85.
V & A/Snowman 1977, no. 013, catalogue p. 98, reproduced.
REFERENCES
Snowman 1953/55, no. 165, 166, reproduced twice.
Snowman 1962/64, no. 182, 183, reproduced twice.
FORBES, April 1, 1972, p. 47, reproduced in color.
Villager/Sears, p. 5.
Nineteenth Century/Snowman, p. 53, reproduced in color.
N.Y. Times/Reif, p. C17.

86. IMPERIAL PARASOL HANDLE

2-1/2 in./65 mm.
ACC. NO. FAB73004

The cursive T-shaped bowenite handle has a gold mount enamelled pink, to one side of which is applied the crowned cypher of the Czarina Alexandra Feodorovna in rose diamonds on an oval white enamel panel within chased gold laurel border beneath a red gold ribbon. Two further chased gold laurel swags are caught by another ribbon tie on the other side, set with a rose diamond and suspending a laurel pendant; chased laurel border below.

PROVENANCE
Czarina Alexandra Feodorovna.
A La Vieille Russie, New York.
EXHIBITION
ALVR 1968, no. 309, catalogue p. 118, reproduced.
REFERENCE
FORBES, June 1, 1974, p. 54, reproduced in color.

87. PINK WHISTLE

1-3/8 in./35 mm.
MARKS: *72*, another mark obscured on loop, scratched *1005A BiM.*
CASE: Original fitted hollowood; 2-1/2 in./60 mm.; lid lining stamped in gold, *Eagle/FABERGÉ/St. Petersburg/ Moscow Odessa.*
ACC. NO. FAB78003

The cylindrical silver whistle is enamelled translucent pink on a guilloche ground. The lip piece and sound-hole are gilt as is the pendant loop.

PROVENANCE
Anon. Sale: Christie's, London, March 1, 1960, Lot 154, catalogue p. 26.

88. PINK HANDLE

2-3/8 in./60 mm.
MARKS: *kokoshnik, 56, BA, kokoshnik* on lower rim; scratched *2217A UKM.* (Aarne).
ACC. NO. FAB76014

The cylindrical gold handle is enamelled a salmon pink with a palmette border chased in green gold above a beaded red gold band. The upper mount is chased in green gold with laurel foliage and a moonstone finial. The handle now has a silver-gilt blade resembling that of a Malay kris, by Tom Scott, which unscrews.

(Appendix D for handle with blade).

PROVENANCE
Wartski, London.
REFERENCE
FORBES, October 1, 1976, p. 112, reproduced in color.

89. *Pink Rocaille Opera Glasses*

Wartski, London.
Lansdell K. Christie, Long Island (Sale: Parke-Bernet, New York, New York, December 7, 1967, Lot 21, catalogue p. 12, reproduced).
A La Vieille Russie, New York.
EXHIBITIONS
Corcoran 1961, no. 72, catalogue p. 46.
Metropolitian 1962-66, no. L.62.8.72.

REFERENCES
Snowman 1962/64, no. 186, reproduced.
Metropolitian Bulletin/McNab Dennis, p. 229, reproduced frontispiece.
Great Private Collections/Snowman, p. 244, reproduced.
Rita Reif, "Glittering Baubles Made for a Czar," *New York Times*, April 23, 1978, p. D24.

89. PINK ROCAILLE OPERA GLASSES

4-1/4 in./105 mm.
MARKS: *FABERGÉ* on lower band; *56 JL, MP* on upper band; scratched *3945.* (Perchin).
CASE: Fitted brown suede; 4-7/8 in./123 mm.; unstamped.
ACC. NO. FAB76012

Both eye glasses and the central strut are enamelled a translucent pink over an engine-turned ground of swag design, applied with rococo scroll and lattice motifs in rose diamonds; all the borders are set with further rose diamonds. With red gold mounts to the horizontal bands.

PROVENANCE
Jan Skala, New York.

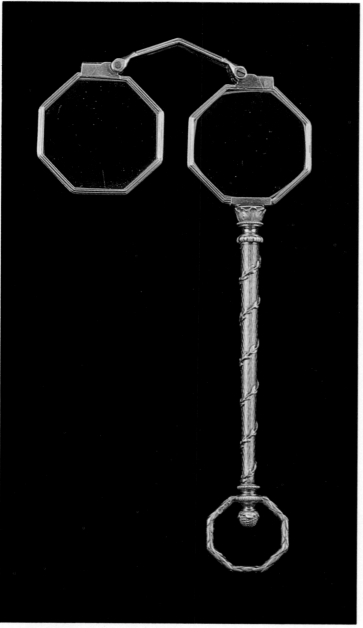

90. Lorgnette

91. Five Buttons

90. LORGNETTE

5-7/8 in./150 mm.
MARKS: *KF, 56 kokoshnik IL* inside bridge; *KF, kokoshnik* on
    loop.
ACC. NO. FAB69002

The mounts are of gold with octagonal glasses, the
cylindrical handle is enamelled pink and chased with
a spiral of green-gold foliage. The chased octagonal
terminal loop has a red-gold pineapple at its center.

PROVENANCE
Mrs. L. D. Hirst-Broadhead (Sale: Sotheby & Co., London,
    December 8, 1969, Lot 107, catalogue p. 45, reproduced
    in color).
EXHIBITION
NYCC/Waterfield 1973, no. 35, catalogue p. 84, repro-
    duced in color p. 85.
REFERENCES
Art at Auction, 1969-1970, New York and London, 1970,
    p. 404, reproduced in color.
FORBES, April 1, 1972, p. 47, reproduced in color.
Villager/Sears, p. 5.
N.Y. Times/Reif, p. C17.

91. FIVE BUTTONS

7/8 in./23 mm.
MARKS: *56, IL, KF* on back; *HH kokoshnik* on pin; scratched
    23823. All on each button.
ACC. NO. FAB76024

The circular gold buttons are each set with a diamond
and three foliate scroll motifs on a panel of translucent turquoise blue enamel with swirl motif, the
narrow white enamel borders are embellished with
gold dots. The loop for attachment has a further
detachable hairpin-shaped gold link.

(See Appendix D for detail of button backs).

PROVENANCE
Anon. Sale: Sotheby Parke Bernet Monaco S.A., Monte
    Carlo, June 25-26, 1976, Lot 636, catalogue p. 151,
    reproduced.
A La Vieille Russie, New York.

92. KNITTING NEEDLES

9-3/8 in./238 mm.
MARKS: HW, 56 on both finials. (Wigström).
ACC. NO. FAB73001

The ebonized wood shafts have cylindrical gold
mounts which are decorated with spiral ornament in
white enamel above chased husk borders. The bun-
shaped blue chalcedony finials are set with a
cabochon ruby in the center of a white enamel
quatrefoil.

PROVENANCE

Anon. Sale: Sotheby & Co., London, February 26, 1973, Lot 179, catalogue p. 30, reproduced Plate VII.

A La Vieille Russie, New York.

REFERENCES

FORBES, August 1, 1974, p. 43, reproduced in color.

N.Y. Times, Reif, p. C17.

93. FESTOONED FAN

8-1/2 in./218 mm. closed.

MARKS: *HW, FABERGÉ, 56 kokoshnik AP* on guard top edge; *kokoshnik AP, HW* inside loop. (Wigström).

ACC. NO. FAB75006

The silk-mounted gauze leaf is inset with a silk panel painted in colors with a *scène gallante*, signed: *A. E. Begnée*, and two small landscapes, the whole sewn with gold and silver sequins and shaped paillettes in foliate and geometric patterns. The base of the mother-of-pearl sticks are pierced and gilt with simple scroll motifs, as is the back guard; the front guard is of gold, enamelled a salmon pink and applied with entwined laurel festoons in chased gold with rose diamond quatrefoils at the intersections, the reeded gold swing handle is set with a rose diamond on each side.

PROVENANCE

Anon. Sale: Christie's, London, November 21, 1938, Lot 29, catalogue p. 7. £6.10s.

Berry-Hill Galleries, London and New York.

Anon. Sale: Christie's, Geneva, November 11, 1975, Lot 233, catalogue p. 59, reproduced Plate 16.

A La Vieille Russie, New York.

REFERENCE

FORBES, October 1, 1976, p. 112, reproduced in color.

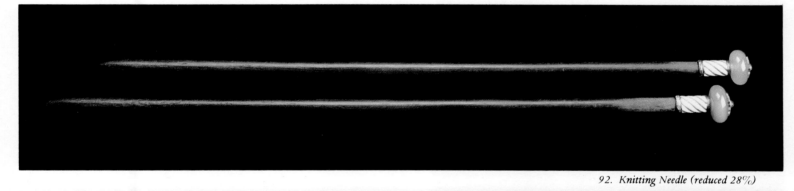

92. Knitting Needle (reduced 28%)

93. Festooned Fan (reduced 53%)

94. Holy Ghost Badge

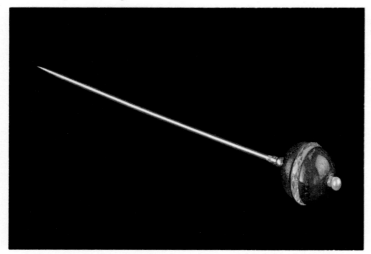

95. Hat Pin

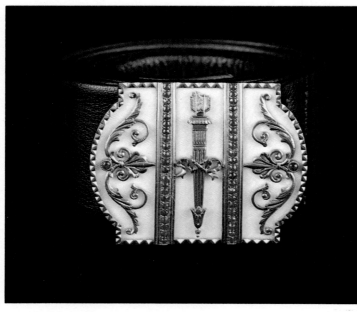

96. Belt Buckle

94. *BADGE OF THE BROTHERHOOD OF THE HOLY GHOST OF THE TRINITY*

3-1/4 in./85 mm.
MARKS: *I.P., kokoshnik, alpha kokoshnik 84* on back; *kokoshnik, I.P.* on pin; *56* on crown. Inscribed in Cyrillic script *Emblem of the Vilna Brotherhood of the Holy Ghost of the Trinity 1909.* (Rappoport).
ACC. NO. FAB67002

The silver-gilt badge has a gold dove on a white enamel cross at the center, which is applied to a blue enamel circle. This in turn rests upon an eight-pointed star applied with the gold initials S.D.V.B. on the alternating silver rays: the whole upon a blue enamel circle. Above all this is wrought the Imperial Crown in gold.

Vilna is a town of northern Russia. The Brotherhood of the Holy Ghost of the Trinity was a very chauvinistic conservative organization which thrived in Czarist Russia.

PROVENANCE
Richard R. Draper, St. Louis.
EXHIBITION
NYCC/Waterfield 1973, no. 38, catalogue p. 88, reproduced p. 89.

95. *HAT PIN*

4 in./102 mm.
MARKS: scratched *2882* on shaft.
ACC. NO. FAB77005

The simple pointed gold shaft emerges from a head conceived of two small hemispheres of lapis-lazuli bisected by a faceted blue sapphire and mounted with a natural pink pearl finial.

PROVENANCE
T. H. Ching, New York.

96. *BELT BUCKLE*

2-1/4 in./58 mm.
MARKS: *KF, 56 kokoshnik* on back.
ACC. NO. FAB73012

The gold buckle is enamelled an opalescent white and divided into three panels by two small gold bands set with rubies. The side panels are applied with gold scroll work and the center with a gold quiver.

This piece, originally made as a belt buckle, was transformed into a brooch and was refitted as a buckle in 1973.

PROVENANCE
Wartski, London.
EXHIBITION
NYCC/Waterfield 1973, no. 36, catalogue p. 86, reproduced in color p. 87.

97. TREFOIL CUFF LINKS

5/8 in./15 mm.
MARKS: *56, kokoshnik alpha*, obscured initials on back;
 FABERGÉ, scratched *15/945* on stick. All on both
 links.
ACC. NO. FAB76003

The shaped triangular gold panels are set with a
single cabochon sapphire within a chased gold laurel
wreath on a panel of translucent white enamel; with
hinged oval retainer on curved attachment.

(See Appendix D for detail of backs).

PROVENANCE
Juvel og Kunst, Copenhagen.
FORBES Magazine (Sale: Sotheby Parke Bernet, New
 York, December 13-14, 1977, Lot 149F, reproduced in
 catalogue).

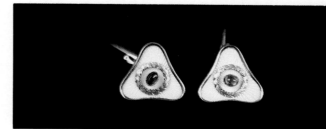

97. Trefoil Cuff Links

98. Admiral Cuff Links

98. ADMIRAL GRAND DUKE ALEXIS CUFF LINKS

3/4 in./18 mm.
MARKS: *A * H, KF* on loop; *kokoshnik 56* on chain. All on
 both links. (Hollming).
ACC. NO. FAB75002

The panels of the gold cuff-links are of shaped-square
form, two of which are set with the crowned cypher
of the Grand Duke Alexis in rose diamonds on a
white enamel ground within rose diamond borders,
the other two are similarly decorated with an anchor.
Each crown is set with two cabochon rubies, each
anchor with one, the latter also with applied thin
gold rope. Four gold links and clasp for attachment.

Until his death in 1909, Grand Duke Alexis was
'General-Admiral' of the Russian Navy during the
reigns of his brother, Alexander III, and nephew,
Nicholas II.

(Appendix D for detail of backs).

PROVENANCE
Grand Duke Alexis Alexandrovitch.
Juvel og Kunst, Copenhagen.

99. CROWN CUFF LINKS

1/2 in./13 mm.
The collection of Malcolm S. Forbes.

The square cuff links are set with Imperial Crowns
embellished with rose diamonds. The borders are
chased with foliage in green gold enclosing panels of
white guilloche enamel. To the backs are fastened
simple gold butterfly mechanisms which fix the cuff
links in place.

(See Appendix D for detail of backs).

EXHIBITION
NYCC/Waterfield 1973, no. 37, catalogue p. 86, reproduced in color p. 87.

99. Crown Cuff Links

100. PINK-EGG CUFF LINKS

1/2 in./12 mm.
MARKS: *72 anchors, HW* on joining loop. All on both links.
 (Wigström).
ACC. NO. FAB74001

The four oviform gold links are enamelled a salmon
pink and engraved with cursive cross bands to
produce a cushion effect. With circular links for
attachment.

PROVENANCE
Anon. Sale: Christie's, Geneva, May 1, 1974, Lot 158,
 catalogue p. 53.
A La Vieille Russie, New York.

100. Pink-Egg Cuff Links

DESK PIECES

While one might question the amount of work done at desks in Czarist Russia, large sums of money were spent on lavish writing accessories. Personal correspondence was a major pastime of the leisured classes, as the prodigious quantity of letters still extant of the last Czarina will testify, and to help with these outpourings, the House of Fabergé created jewelled pens, handseals carved of semiprecious stones, diamond-studded blotters, jade pencil holders, and the like. The firm also made handsome matching desk garnitures, but for the most part, these are less imaginative and brilliantly crafted than individually conceived pieces such as those illustrated on the following pages.

101. Presentation Document Folder (reduced 29%)

101. PRESENTATION DOCUMENT FOLDER

12-1/2 in./335 mm.
MARKS: *FABERGÉ, anchors 88, MP on border. (Perchin).*
ACC. NO. FAB74002

The front cover of the pale cream-colored leather folder has an applied silver-gilt ornament. In the center are the crowned cyphers of Czar Nicholas II and Czarina Alexandra set with rose diamonds within a floral wreath, finely chased and bound with a ribbon inscribed in Russian: *From the City of St. Petersburg.* This is within an oval of Gothic motif and outer rectangular molded border, with foliate spirals of classical inspiration within the spandrels. On the lower border are chased the arms of the City of St. Petersburg within branches of oak and laurel; the angles are chased with acanthus foliage. The interior is lined with ivory-colored watered silk. The folder was commissioned by the City of St. Petersburg for their Imperial Majesties but was never presented.

PROVENANCE
The City of St. Petersburg for their Imperial Majesties Nicholas II and Alexandra prior to 1903. Never presented.
Anon. Sale: Christie's, Geneva, May 1, 1974, Lot 177, catalogue p. 59, reproduced Plate 37.
EXHIBITION
"East Side House Winter Antiques Show, Special Exhibition—Great Private Collections," Seventh Regiment Armory, New York, January 28-February 5, 1978, no. 31, catalogue p. 33.
REFERENCE
Home News/Cook p. C1.

102. TWENTY-FIFTH ANNIVERSARY CLOCK

6 in./166 mm.
MARKS: *kokoshnik 91, HW on back; HW, 91 on strut; scratched 18008, 543E, NMM (Wigström).*
ACC. NO. FAB69008.

The nephrite panel is applied with a silver-gilt cartouche enamelled a translucent pink within a border of chased laurel foliage in green-gold set with rose diamond florettes at intervals, red-gold ribbons and below the letters XXV. The clock face is of palest blue translucent enamel with gold hands and pearl borders, the back and strut are of silver-gilt.

This was made for a twenty-fifth wedding anniversary (silver wedding) probably on a commission from London, since 91 zolotniks was up to the standard of the London Assay Office, Russian silver being normally either 84 or 88.

PROVENANCE
Two nuns from whom it was purchased by Wartski, London on April 22, 1950.
Mr. and Mrs. C. J. Byrne (Sale: Sotheby & Co., London, December 8, 1969, Lot 86, catalogue p. 39, reproduced opposite).

EXHIBITIONS
NYCC/Waterfield 1973, no. 27, catalogue p. 76, reproduced in color p. 78.
V & A/Snowman 1977, no. L5, catalogue p. 72.
REFERENCES
Snowman 1953, no. 130, reproduced.
Snowman 1962/64, no. 142, reproduced.
Art at Auction, 1969-70, New York and London, 1970, p. 402, reproduced.
FORBES, March 15, 1971, p. 58, reproduced in color.

103. HVIDØRE SEAL

2-1/4 in./55 mm.
MARKS: *56 anchors, MP, FABERGÉ near base; scratched 50050. (Perchin).*
CASE: Brown suede draw bag.
ACC. NO. FAB77001

103. Hvidøre Seal

The oviform nephrite handle is partly enveloped in a gold cagework pierced and chased in the rococo style with flowers, latticework and scrolls, the reed and leaf mount is surmounted by wave ornament and encloses the circular cornelian matrix cut with the word HVIDØRE. The inscription is explained by Prince Vassili Romanov,

> *My late Grandmother, the Empress Dowager Maria Feodorovna and her sister Queen Alexandra bought a villa in 1907 outside Copenhagen with large gardens on to the seashore and named it HVIDØRE which means 'white ear' for a strip of beach that stuck out into the sea resembling an ear. So the seal has that name.*

(Appendix D for sisters at Hvidøre and detail of matrix).

PROVENANCE
Czarina Maria Feodorovna.
Grand Duchess Xenia, Windsor, her daughter.
Prince Vassili Romanov, California, her son.
William Beadleston, New York, his son-in-law.
EXHIBITION
"Fabergé, Goldsmith to the Russian Court," M.H. de Young Memorial Museum, San Francisco, 1964, no. 104, catalogue p. 32, 55, reproduced p. 32.

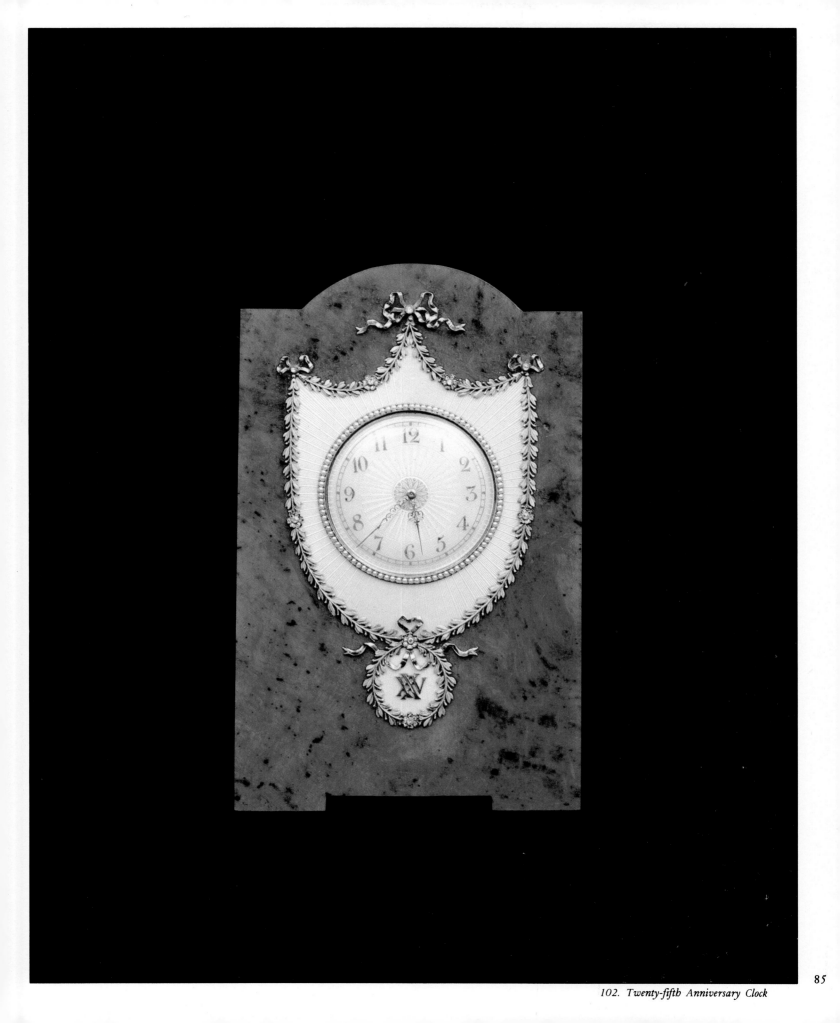

102. Twenty-fifth Anniversary Clock

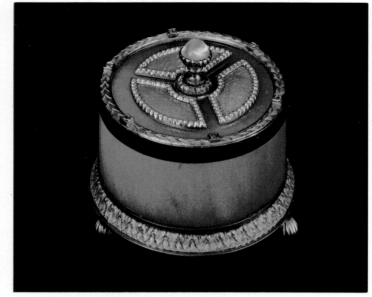

104. Round Bell Push

104. ROUND BELL PUSH

2-1/4 in./58 mm.
MARKS: FABERGÉ, kokoshnik 56, MP, kokoshnik on edge.
(Perchin).
ACC. NO. FAB76009

The cylindrical body is of a grayish-green jade with gold mounts, those to the base are chased with palmettes in green gold, those to the cover with laurel set with six rose diamonds at intervals. The top has three sections of salmon pink enamel within seed pearl borders, with rose diamond border to the pushbutton which has a moonstone finial. The whole rests on three reeded spherical gold feet.

PROVENANCE
Juvel og Kunst, Copenhagen.
REFERENCE
FORBES, May 29, 1978, p. 97, reproduced in color.

105. Oval Bell Push

105. OVAL BELL PUSH

2-3/4 in./71 mm.
CASE: Fitted gray morocco; 4-3/8 in./112 mm.; lid lining stamped in gold Crest/By Appointment to/H. M. The Queen/Jewellers/WARTSKI/138 Regent St./London and Llandudno.
ACC. NO. FAB65005

The oval pale green jade panel is set with a gold plaque enamelled a translucent white and applied with a laurel wreath chased in green-gold, held by three small rose diamonds and pierced with a red-gold arrow. The pushpiece is a carbuncle and it stands on gold bun feet.

PROVENANCE
Anon. Sale: Sotheby & Co., London, November 9, 1964, Lot 13, catalogue p. 6, reproduced opposite.
Wartski, London.
EXHIBITION
NYCC/Waterfield 1973, no. 30, catalogue p. 80, reproduced p. 81.
REFERENCES
FORBES, October 1, 1968, p. 65, reproduced in color.
Home News/Cook, p. C2.
FORBES, May 29, 1978, p. 97, reproduced in color.

106. CARD HOLDER

3 in./75 mm. high.
MARKS: FABERGÉ, MP, 56 kokoshnik on base band; scratched 3239. (Perchin).
ACC. NO. FAB76013

Translucent sheets of nephrite are mounted en cage with red-gold corner bands to form this narrow rectangular card or letter holder. The bands are chased with a green-gold laurel border and the ensemble rests on reeded red-gold bun feet.

PROVENANCE
A La Vieille Russie, New York.
REFERENCE
FORBES, May 1, 1977, p. 102, reproduced in color.

107. PEN REST

6-1/2 in./168 mm.
MARKS: FABERGÉ, 56 anchor, MP on left edge; anchor on right edge; scratched 56200. (Perchin).
ACC. NO. FAB73006

The bowenite is carved as a half-cylinder mounted in gold which is enamelled with scarlet lozenges between white pellets. It rests on two bracket feet of the Greek key pattern supported by semi-circular bands.

PROVENANCE
A La Vieille Russie, New York.
REFERENCE
FORBES, September 15, 1974, p. 114, reproduced in color.

106. Card Holder

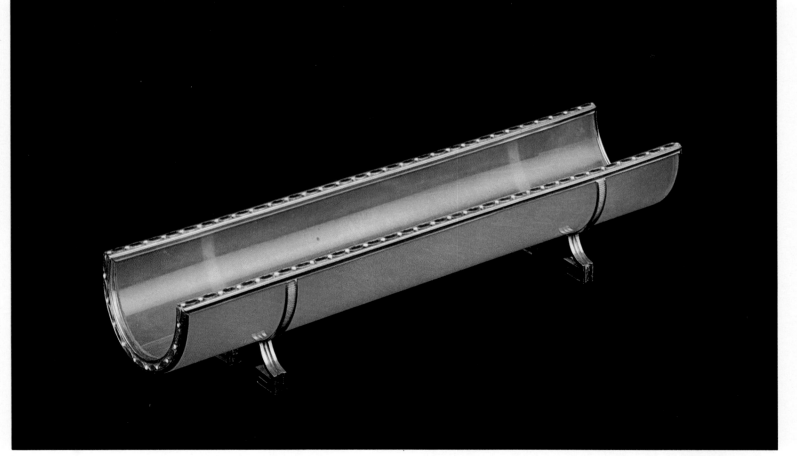

107. Pen Rest

108. NEPHRITE DESK PAD

5-1/2 in./126 mm.
MARKS: *Eagle K. FABERGÉ, kokoshnik* on top edge; *Eagle K. FABERGÉ, 84 kokoshnik* on bottom edge; *kokoshnik IL, KF, 56* on swag; *56* on ribbon; scratched *27372*.
ACC. NO. FAB76032

The hinged cover of the plain rectangular silver-gilt pad is set with a panel of nephrite within a white enamel border. The panel has an applied laurel wreath chased in green gold suspended on red gold ribbons from a rod with pineapple finials, which also suspends a longer swag of laurel. Below is set a beribboned gold quiver. The reeded hinge has cabochon pink stone finials within foliate collets.

(Appendix D for detail of pencil).

PROVENANCE
Jan Skala, New York.

109. GRAND DUCHESS OLGA PAPER KNIFE

9 in./228 mm.
MARKS: *FABERGÉ, 56 kokoshnik JL* on finial; scratched *6245*.
CASE: Original fitted hollywood; 10 in./250 mm.; stamped in black *Eagle/FABERGÉ/St. Petersburg/Moscow Odessa*.
ACC. NO. FAB76005

The tapering nephrite blade of the knife is enclosed at one end by a gold hood, enamelled on one side in scarlet. This panel has an oval aperture enclosing a portrait of the Grand Duchess Olga, below which is set a rose diamond in a red gold bow. The curved border is chased with green gold laurel foliage. Grand Duchess Olga was a sister of Czar Nicholas II.

PROVENANCE
Grand Duchess Olga Alexandrovna.
Anon. Sale: Sotheby & Co., London, April 28, 1975, Lot 171, catalogue p. 19, reproduced opposite.
Juvel og Kunst, Copenhagen.
REFERENCE
FORBES, May 1, 1977, p. 102, reproduced in color.

110. SERPENT PEN

7 in./177 excluding nib.
MARKS: *56 anchors, MP, FABERGÉ* on mount exterior; *MP, anchors* inside mount; scratched *1244*. (Perchin).
ACC. NO. FAB65009

The nephrite handle has reeded gold mounts and is entwined at either end with serpents of gold set with rose diamonds, each head with a cabochon ruby.

PROVENANCE
Bentley & Co., London.
EXHIBITION
NYCC/Waterfield 1973, no. 29, catalogue p. 78, reproduced p. 79.

REFERENCES
FORBES, October 1, 1968, p. 65, reproduced in color.
Esquire, p. 139, reproduced in color.

111. PERPETUAL DESK CALENDAR

5-3/4 in./143 mm.
MARKS: *FABERGÉ, MP, anchors 88* on bottom edge; *anchors 88, MP* on strut. (Perchin).
ACC. NO. FAB65008

111. Perpetual Desk Calendar

The rectangular nephrite panel is set with four moonstones at the corners and three moonstones on the knobs either side which turn the dates for the calendar. With chased gold laurel foliage applied about the central aperture.

PROVENANCE
Bentley & Co., London.
EXHIBITION
NYCC/Waterfield 1973, no. 28, catalogue p. 78, reproduced p. 79.
REFERENCES
FORBES, October 1, 1968, p. 65, reproduced in color.
Esquire, reproduced in color p. 139.
Home News/Cook, p. C2.

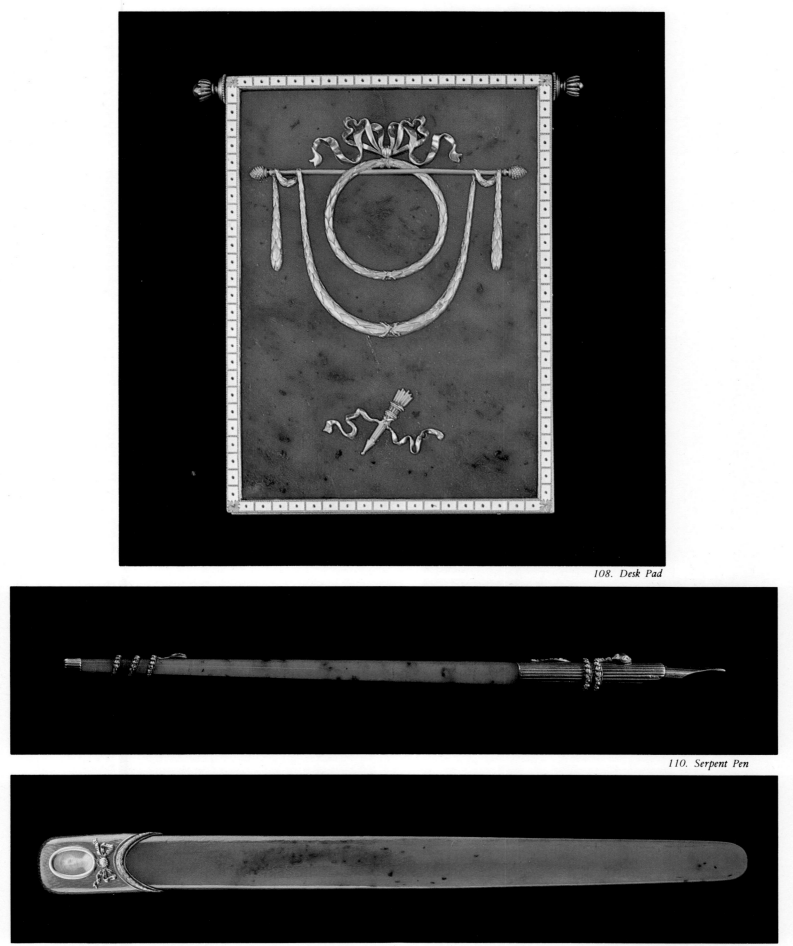

108. Desk Pad

110. Serpent Pen

109. Olga Paper Knife (reduced 18%)

89

112. BOOK MARKER

2-7/8 in./73 mm.
MARKS: *FABERGÉ, 56 anchors, MP* on loop; scratched *182ABI/-/-.* (Perchin).
ACC. NO. FAB69010

The leaf-shaped marker of crystal with a gold clip behind. The handle top is enamelled a translucent pink and is set with a pearl.

PROVENANCE
Mrs. L. D. Hirst-Broadhead (Sale: Sotheby & Co., London, December 8, 1969, Lot 101, catalogue p. 43, reproduced).
EXHIBITION
NYCC/Waterfield 1973, no. 33, catalogue p. 82, reproduced in color p. 83.
REFERENCE
FORBES, July 15, 1971, p. 54, reproduced in color.

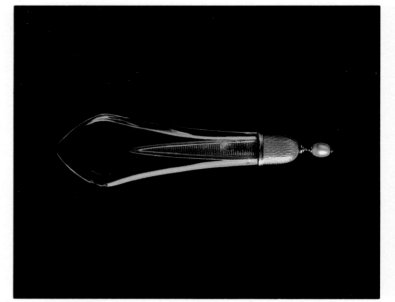

112. Book Marker

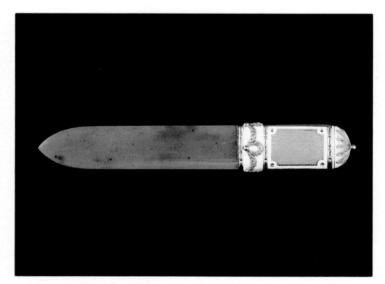

113. Nephrite Paper Knife

114. MAGNIFYING GLASS

3-1/16 in./78 mm.
MARKS: *kokoshnik 56, HW* on edge; scratched *15893.* (Wigström).
ACC. NO. FAB69009

The single circular glass within gold mounts chased with green-gold foliage, the red enamel handle joined between green-gold foliage circlets.

PROVENANCE
Mrs. L. D. Hirst-Broadhead (Sale: Sotheby & Co., London, December 8, 1969, Lot 100, catalogue p. 42, reproduced).
EXHIBITION
NYCC/Waterfield 1973, no. 32, catalogue p. 82, reproduced in color p. 83.
REFERENCE
FORBES, July 15, 1971, p. 54, reproduced in color.

113. NEPHRITE PAPER KNIFE

3-3/8 in./98 mm.
MARKS: scratched *B181* (?).
ACC. NO. FAB69003

The gold handle is enamelled a translucent salmon-pink between opaque white borders, with chased swags of foliage in green gold. The blade is of nephrite.

PROVENANCE
Mrs. L. D. Hirst-Broadhead (Sale: Sotheby & Co., London, December 8, 1969, Lot 108, catalogue p. 45, reproduced in color opposite).
EXHIBITION
NYCC/Waterfield 1973, no. 31, catalogue p. 82, reproduced in color p. 83.
REFERENCES
Art at Auction, 1969-70, New York and London, 1970, p. 403, reproduced in color.
FORBES, July 15, 1971, reproduced in color p. 54.

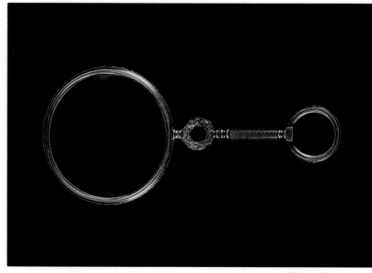

114. Magnifying Glass

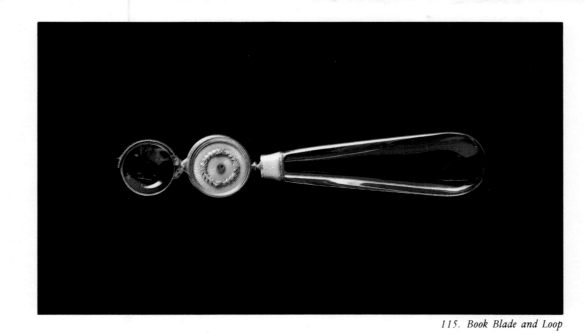

115. Book Blade and Loop

115. BOOK BLADE AND LOOP

4 in./102 mm.
Marks: *MP, anchors* on loop, scratched *52664.* (Perchin).
Acc. no. FAB76015

The circular translucent pink enamel panels are each set with a cabochon ruby within a chased green gold laurel circlet with red gold ribbon ties, with reeded mounts and hinged glass. The flat tapering crystal handle has a small gold mount enamelled pink and is probably a replacement.

Provenance
H. M. King Farouk (Sale, by order of the Egyptian Government: Sotheby & Co., Cairo, March 10-13, 17-20, 1954, Lot 117, catalogue p. 24).
Robert Strauss, Stonehurst, England (Sale: Christie's, London, March 9, 1976, Lot 12, catalogue p. 12, reproduced in color p. 13).
Wartski, London.

116. LAPIS LAZULI SEAL

3-1/2 in./90 mm.
Acc. no. FAB73009

The slender cylindrical lapis lazuli handle is a very deep blue with gold inclusions, the hemispherical base of a slightly lighter blue. The wide gold mount is set with three rose diamonds on rectangular peach-colored enamel panels within white enamel borders embellished with six green dots; with outer borders of rose diamonds.

Provenance
Anon. Sale: Christie's, London, November 13, 1973, Lot 134, catalogue p. 32, reproduced Plate 15.
The Fine Art Society, London.
A La Vieille Russie, New York.
Reference
N.Y. Times/Reif p. C17.

116. Lapis Seal

HOUSEHOLD OBJECTS

Household objects is a catch-all heading under which to place a diversity of pieces which do not quite fit elsewhere. Some things like the menu holders, silver ceremonial kovsh and card-suit ash-trays are undeniably functional pieces. Others like the helmet cup, miniature samovar and eagle vase could almost as justifiably have been placed among the fantasies. But, whatever the heading, the objects in this section share with their counterparts the same brilliance of execution and balance of material that are the hallmarks of the House of Fabergé.

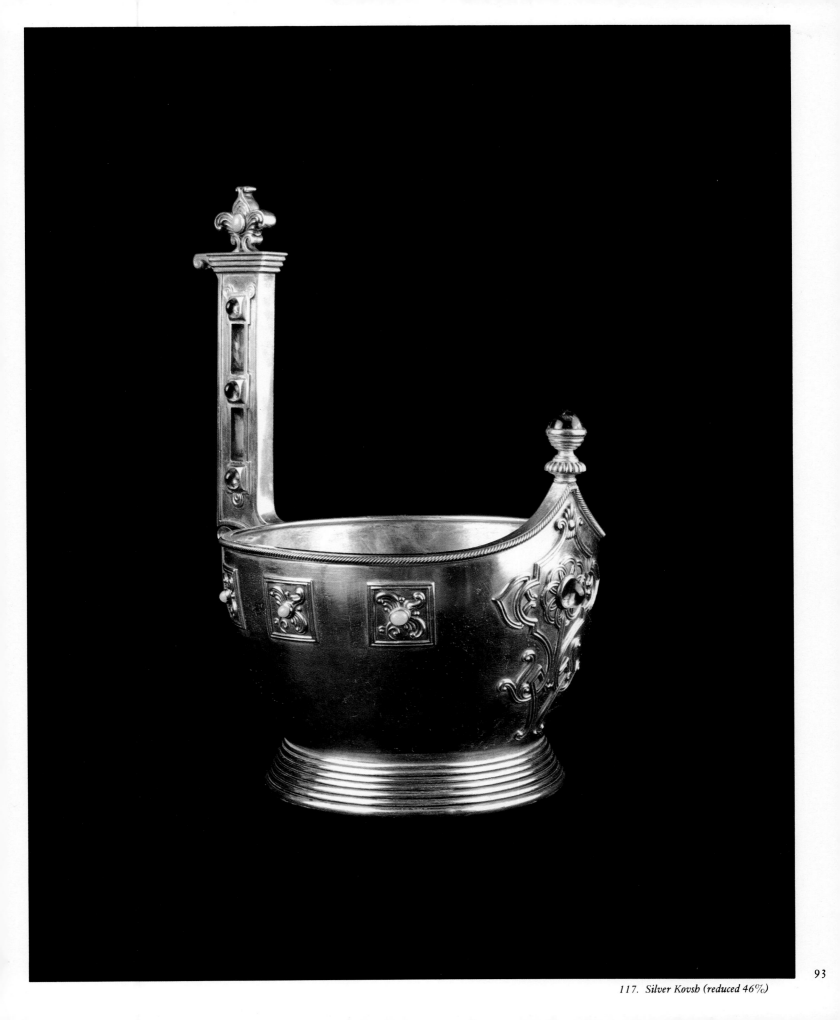

117. Silver Kovsh (reduced 46%)

118. Miniature Samovar

117. *LARGE SILVER KOVSH*

12-5/8 in./320mm.
MARKS: *84 kokoshnik IL, Eagle FABERGÉ* on base; scratched *22203.* Later engraved in gothic initials and Roman script *Z · M · C/Remembering the Caucasus/May 1920.*
ACC. NO. 74005

The hemispherical silver bowl is chased with eight foliate scroll motifs, each set with a moonstone or dyed agate within a square cartouche. One end is raised with a foiled cabochon amethyst, the body below set with another large amethyst within formal floral device. The vertical handle is pierced with two rectangles flanked by cabochon amethysts, chased with an exotic flower below; the bud-shaped finial is set with two moonstones. The rim is corded and the foot broadly reeded.

PROVENANCE
The Dvani Family, Georgia, Russia.
Zenas Marshal Crane of Crane Paper. Gift of the Dvani Family for his assistance in getting them out of Russia, May 1920.
Zenas Crane Colt, his nephew.
Zenas Marshall Crane Colt, New York, his son.
Bianca Redden Colt, New York, his wife.
REFERENCE
FORBES, December 1, 1976, p. 94, reproduced in color.

118. *MINIATURE SAMOVAR*

3-3/4 in./96mm.
MARKS: *AN, 88 kokoshnik* on base edge; *88* on fretwork; scratched *6936.* (Nevalainen).
ACC. NO. FAB77003

The samovar is of silver-gilt, the almost spherical body with tap to one side, the crown-shaped ivory handle of which turns, the hollow turret above unscrews and has a pierced gallery; all the handles and knobs are of ivory. The square base rests on four reeded bun feet.

An almost identical miniature samovar in gold by Wigström was sold at Christie's, Geneva on April 26, 1978, Lot 114 and is reproduced in the catalogue.

PROVENANCE
Anon. Sale: Sotheby Parke Bernet, New York, May 25, 1977, Lot 459, reproduced in catalogue.
Jan Skala, New York.
REFERENCES
N.Y. Times/Reif, p. C17.
"Important Russian Works of Art," Christie's, Geneva, April 26, 1978, p. 114.

119. Miniature Coin Tankard

120. Eagle Vase

119. MINIATURE COIN TANKARD

3-1/4 in./85 mm.
MARKS: *56 anchors, EK* on base; scratched *150.0.*
  (Kollin).
ACC. NO. FAB69004

A simple gold tankard with gadrooned borders, the cover set with a gold 5 ruble coin of Catherine the Great, 1783, the sides with eight 5 ruble pieces of 1779 except one of 1758 and with four 2 ruble pieces of 1777. A cabochon sapphire is set at the thumbpiece and another at the base of the scroll handle.

PROVENANCE
Anon. Sale: Sotheby & Co., London, December 8, 1969, Lot 111, catalogue p. 46, reproduced opposite.
EXHIBITIONS
NYCC/Waterfield 1973, no. 49, catalogue p. 104, reproduced in color p. 105.
V & A/Snowman 1977, no. L6, p. 72.
REFERENCES
FORBES, January 1, 1971, p. 34, reproduced in color.
George Crossette, "Coins," *World Topics Year Book*, Lake Bluff, Illinois, 1972, p. 31, reproduced in color.

120. EAGLE VASE

4-1/8 in./105 mm.
MARKS: *AT, anchors, 56* on base; *AT anchors, 84* under eagle wing. (Thielemann).
ACC. NO. FAB69012

The gold vase is decorated in blue, turquoise and red *plique-à-jour* enamel on a matted gold ground set at intervals with alternating rose diamonds and rubies. The stem is chased in silver as an eagle, the base is of 'samorodok' gold with a border of blue *plique-à-jour* scrolls.

PROVENANCE
Anon. Sale: Parke-Bernet, New York, December 2-3, 1969, Lot 240, catalogue p. 240, reproduced opposite and on cover in color.
EXHIBITION
NYCC/Waterfield 1973, no. 39, catalogue p. 90, reproduced in color p. 91.
REFERENCES
Art at Auction, 1969-70, New York and London, 1970, p. 401, reproduced in color.
FORBES, August 1, 1970, p. 32, reproduced in color.

95

121. Pair of Vodka Cups

122. Helmet Cup

123. Fish Charka

121. PAIR OF VODKA CUPS

1-7/8in./48mm.
Marks (cup with rubies): *FABERGÉ, MP, kokoshnik, 56*
   on base; scratched *2465D, HMM.* (Perchin).
Marks (cup with sapphires): *FABERGÉ, MP, kokoshnik*
   56 on base. (Perchin).
Acc. no. (with rubies): FAB65012
Acc. no. (with sapphires): FAB65010

The reeded gold cups are decorated with alternate
bands of green and red gold, the terminals of the
double-scroll handles are set with cabochon rubies
and sapphires respectively.

Provenance (with rubies)
Wartski, London.
Provenance (with sapphires)
Anon. Sale: Sotheby & Co., London, December 8, 1951, Lot
   129.
H.M. King Farouk (Sale, by order of the Egyptian Govern-
   ment: Sotheby & Co., Cairo, March 10-13, 17-20, 1957,
   Lot 119, catalogue p. 24).
Major W. Heaford Daubney (Sale: Christie's London,
   November 14, 1961, Lot 169, catalogue p. 34, repro-
   duced opposite).
Bentley & Co., London.
Exhibition (both)
NYCC/Waterfield 1973, no. 41, catalogue p. 92, repro-
   duced in color p. 93.
Reference (both)
FORBES, December 1, 1972, p. 75, reproduced in color.

122. HELMET CUP

3-1/4in./85mm.
Marks: *kokoshnik 84, kokoshnik, FABERGÉ* on rear rim;
   kokoshnik 84 on eagle base.
Acc. no. FAB74005

The silver-gilt helmet of the Cavalier Guards is
surmounted by a chased silver Imperial Eagle on a
shaped cartouche, the front has the applied silver Star
of the Order of St. Andrew with enamelled center.

The chased silver chin strap has a simple fastening and one enamelled cockade hinge plate. When inverted, the helmet serves as a vodka cup.

(Appendix D for helmet inverted).

PROVENANCE
A La Vieille Russie, New York.
Anon. Sale: Sotheby Parke Bernet, New York, May 16-18, 1974, Lot 462, catalogue p. 116, reproduced.
EXHIBITION
ALVR 1968, no. 75, catalogue p. 75.
REFERENCES
FORBES, February 1, 1976, p. 64, reproduced in color.
N.Y. Times/Reif, p. C17.

123. FISH CHARKA

3-1/2 in./88 mm.
MARKS: *anchors 56, MP, FABERGÉ* on base rim; *MP* on inside rim; scratched *43596, 5886, 25n.* (Perchin).
CASE: Fitted grey morocco; 4-7/8 in./125 mm.; lid lining stamped in gold *Crest/By Appointment/WARTSKI/LTD/ 138 Regent St./London W1/and Llandudno.*
ACC. NO. FAB77004

The outside of the gold bowl is chased as flowing water with six applied fish in white and red gold, the eyes set with rubies, the whole in the Japanese taste. The foot has six chased gold scallop shells and the handle is set with a gold ruble of the Empress Elizabeth I, 1756, the top of the handle is set with a cabochon sapphire.

PROVENANCE
Anon. Sale: Sotheby Parke Bernet, London, June 20, 1977, Lot 205, catalogue p. 58, reproduced in color.
Wartski, London.
REFERENCE
Art at Auction 1976-77, New York and London, 1977, p. 261, reproduced in color.

124. DECANTER STOPPER

4-1/2 in./115 mm.
9-3/4 in./247 mm. with decanter.
MARKS: *BA, JL kokoshnik 88, FABERGÉ* under base rim. (Aarne).
ACC. NO. FAB76030

This utilitarian piece is formed of a handsome sculpted silver double-headed Imperial Eagle perched on a silver globe rising from a fluted base, below which is mounted a fitted cork.

The stopper is a replacement for a crystal decanter made during the first quarter of the nineteenth century at the Imperial Glass Factory in St. Petersburg. The decanter is decorated on one side with a portrait of Alexander I framed in a laurel wreath and on the other with his crowned monogram similarly framed.

PROVENANCE
Anon. Sale (Sotheby Parke Bernet, New York, November 30, 1972, Lot 39, reproduced above Lot 172).
A La Vieille Russie, New York.

124. Decanter Stopper

Two fringed gold swags are suspended from cabochon rubies set on each side with loops through which pass tasselled ropes, each of the four tassels set with a band of rose diamonds. On one side beneath the swag is an applied gold Imperial Eagle set with rose diamonds about a central diamond.

PROVENANCE
A La Vieille Russie, New York.
REFERENCE
FORBES, October 16, 1978, p. 125, reproduced in color.

125. Imperial Cylinder Vase

126. STYLE-MODERNE KOVSH

5 in./128mm
CASE: Original fitted hollywood; 6 in./153 mm.; stamped in black *Eagle S. Petersburg/Moscow London*.
ACC. NO. FAB65006

The simple bowl is carved from a single piece of nephrite, the gold handle is enamelled a translucent white and set on both sides with a pink-foiled gray moonstone, another moonstone is set in the screw attachment on the inside of the bowl.

The handle is a highly stylized form derived from the fabulous bird of Russian folklore.

PROVENANCE
Wartski, London.
EXHIBITION
NYCC/Waterfield 1973, no. 48, catalogue p. 102, reproduced p. 103.
REFERENCE
FORBES, October 1, 1972, p. 64, reproduced in color.

127. OVAL RHODONITE DISH

6-3/4 in./170mm.
MARKS: *FA, 56 AP*, on both ribbons; scratched *15871.* (Afanassiev).
ACC. NO. FAB69006

The simple oval dish is of rhodonite, the gold ribbon handles at each end enclose within white enamelled mounts a silver ruble, one dated 1751 and the other 1756. The obverse fields of these are enamelled green and bear the image of the Czarina Elizabeth I.

PROVENANCE
Mrs. Isabella Catt.
Wartski, London.
Anon. Sale: Sotheby & Co., London, December 8, 1969, Lot 82, catalogue p. 37, reproduced opposite.
EXHIBITION
NYCC/Waterfield 1973, no. 46, catalogue p. 98, reproduced in color p. 99.
REFERENCES
Snowman 1953, no. 88, reproduced.
Snowman 1962/64, no. 99, reproduced.
FORBES, May 1, 1971, p. 38, reproduced in color.

125. IMPERIAL CYLINDER VASE

4-5/8 in./117mm.
MARKS: *HW, 56* on left festoon; *56 kokoshnik JL* on right festoon. (Wigström).
ACC. NO. FAB76011

The cylindrical nephrite body of the vase or spill holder is cut with the stepped base and slightly flaring lip.

126. Style-Moderne Kovsh

127. Oval Rhodonite Dish

128. SQUARE BOWENITE DISH

2-7/8 in./74 mm.
MARKS: *kokoshnik, HW, kokoshnik* on rim; engraved in Roman capital letters *FABERGÉ.* (Wigström).
CASE: Original fitted hollywood; 4 in./102 mm.; stamped in black *Eagle/FABERGÉ/St. Petersburg/Moscow London.*
ACC. NO. FAB00001

The square bowenite dish has a gold rim enamelled white with purplish-blue at the corners.

PROVENANCE
Wartski, London.
EXHIBITION
NYCC/Waterfield 1973, no. 44, catalogue p. 94, reproduced in color p. 95.
REFERENCES
FORBES, June 15, 1972, p. 64, reproduced in color.
Vogue Italia/Clay, reproduced in color p. 131.

128. Square Bowenite Dish

129. ROUND BOWENITE DISH

3-1/2 in./89 mm.
MARKS: *MP, 56 kokoshnik JL* on festoons; *MP* inside rim; scratched *6133.* (Perchin).
ACC. NO. FAB76025

The circular dish is cut from a single piece of pale green bowenite which flares toward the base. The rim is chased with green gold laurel and below it are set eight cabochon rubies suspending green gold laurel swags.

PROVENANCE
A Lady of Title (Sale: Christie's Geneva, May 1, 1974, Lot 211, catalogue p. 71, reproduced Plate 46).
A La Vieille Russie, New York.
REFERENCES
Home News/Cook, p. C2.
FORBES, May 1, 1977, p. 102, reproduced in color.

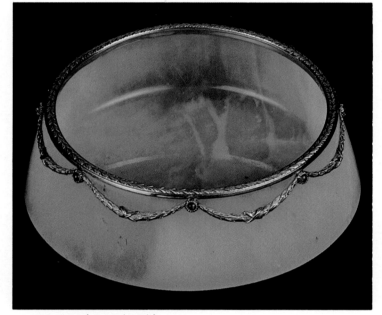

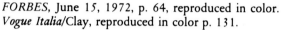

129. Round Bowenite Dish

130. CIRCULAR PINK AGATE DISH

2-3/4 in./79 mm.
MARKS: *HW, kokoshnik 56* on rim; scratched *12311.* (Wigström).
CASE: Fitted gray morocco; 4-3/4 in./110 mm.; lid lining stamped in gold *Crest/By Appointment to/H. M. The Queen/Jewellers/WARTSKI/138 Regent St./London and Llandudno.*
ACC. NO. FAB65004

The circular aventurine quartz dish has a gold rim enamelled in green with laurel and engraved with ribbon ties.

PROVENANCE
Wartski, London.
EXHIBITION
NYCC/Waterfield 1973, no. 45, catalogue p. 96, reproduced p. 97.
REFERENCE
FORBES, October 1, 1972, p. 64, reproduced in color.

130. Circular Pink Agate Dish

131. Miniature Nephrite Kovsh

132. STRIATED AGATE KOVSH

4-1/2 in./112 mm.
MARKS: *FABERGÉ, 56 anchors, MP partly obscured,
under handle; scratched 56483.* (Perchin).
ACC. NO. FAB76020

The oval bowl is carved from a single piece of
translucent brown agate with golden bands and black
cloud effects. The trefoil gold handle is enamelled
green within narrow white borders and applied with
formal flowers enamelled blue, orange and yellow
about a diamond in a banded black enamel collet. A
single rose diamond is set below the triangular panel
on the rim of the bowl.

PROVENANCE
Anon. Sale: Sotheby Parke Bernet, New York, May 20,
    1976, Lot 260, reproduced in catalogue in color Plate
    VII.
A La Vieille Russie, New York.
REFERENCE
Art at Auction, 1975-76, New York and London, 1976, p.
    259, reproduced in color.

133. Art Nouveau Match-Holder

131. MINIATURE NEPHRITE KOVSH

2-1/2 in./65 mm.
CASE: Fitted gray morocco; 4-1/8 in./105 mm.; lid lining
    stamped in silver *A La Vieille Russie/781 Fifth Avenue.*
ACC. NO. 76026

The boat-shaped bowl is of a pale green nephrite; the
gold handle is enamelled a deep red within rose
diamond borders. A single pearl is set below within
the bowl.

PROVENANCE
Lansdell K. Christie, Long Island.
A La Vieille Russie, New York.
EXHIBITION
Metropolitan 1962-66, no. L.62.8.160.
REFERENCE
Metropolitan Bulletin/McNab Dennis, p. 234, no. 8, repro-
duced.

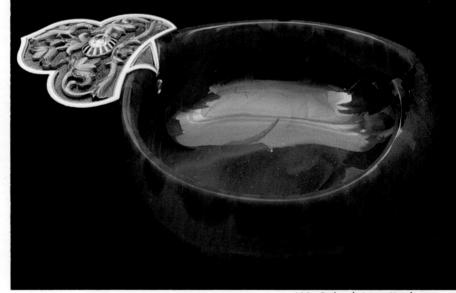

132. Striated Agate Kovsh

133. ART NOUVEAU MATCH-HOLDER

2-5/8 in./68 mm.
MARKS: *HW, 56* in foliage; *FABERGÉ* on edge;
    scratched *7664.* (Wigström).
ACC. NO. FAB00002

The tall octagonal dark gray jasper bowl is encased by
a gold cagework chased as red hot pokers, the heads
set with three olivines, and triple flower-heads set
with rubies, on a stem of eight scrolls, those chased
with lions' masks at the base terminate at the foot
with a leaf set with an olivine, they alternate with
those chased with dolphins, the tails curled and raised
to support the cup.

EXHIBITION
NYCC/Waterfield 1973, no. 40, catalogue p. 92, repro-
    duced in color p. 93.
REFERENCE
FORBES, December 1, 1972, p. 75, reproduced in color.

134. Cornflower Vase

PROVENANCE
Richard B. Draper, St. Louis.
EXHIBITION
NYCC/Waterfield 1973, no. 42, catalogue p. 94, repro-
    duced in color p. 95.
REFERENCES
FORBES, June 15, 1972, p. 64, reproduced in color.
Vogue Italia/Clay, reproduced in color p. 131.

135. CARD-SUIT ASHTRAYS

SPADE: 3-1/4 in./83 mm.
HEART: 2-3/4 in./70 mm.
DIAMOND: 3-5/8 in./92 mm.
CLUB: 3-1/4 in./83 mm.
MARKS: *84 kokoshnik JL, Eagle FABERGÉ* on bottom of
    all; *56, KF, kokoshnik* on inside rim of all; *56, KF,
    kokoshnik* on outside edge of two; two scratched, *26535.*
CASE: Original fitted hollywood; 6-3/4 in./72 mm.; lid
    lining stamped in gold *Eagle/K. FABERGÉ/Moscow/St.
    Petersburg, Odessa.*
ACC. NO. FAB73003

These ashtrays for bridge or other card games are of
silver lined with gold, cast in the form of a club, a
diamond, a heart and a spade, the flat rims painted
with thin ribbon ties and the relevant suit in black or
red on a translucent white guilloche enamel ground,
with reeded borders.

PROVENANCE
Mrs. Hugh J. Chisholm, Jr.
Anon. Sale: Parke-Bernet, New York, October 27-28,
    1970, Lot 701, catalogue p. 335, reproduced.
A La Vieille Russie, New York.
EXHIBITION
"Fabergé, Goldsmith to the Russian Court," M. H. de
    Young Memorial Museum, San Francisco, 1964, no.
    161, catalogue p. 62.
REFERENCE
FORBES, December 15, 1977, p. 80, reproduced in color.

136. FOUR MENU HOLDERS

2-3/8 in./61mm.
MARKS: *Eagle FABERGÉ, AN, 91 kokoshnik AP,* scratched
    14435 on back. All on each holder. (Nevalainen).
ACC. NO. FAB76028

The arched rectangular silver-gilt panels are
enamelled a pale translucent blue over a sunburst
within reed and tie borders; the oblong stepped
hollywood bases are set with a band of silver-gilt
beading.

The 91 would indicate that these menu holders were
made for the English market but it is unusual not to
find the associated English import marks. The
Fabergé mark is probably counterfeit as Nevalainen
worked in St. Petersburg.

PROVENANCE
Mrs. R. L. Cameron (Sale: Christie's, London, March 18,
    1975, Lot 161, catalogue p. 32, reproduced Plate 19).
Wartski, London.

134. CORNFLOWER VASE

8-3/4 in./220mm.
CASE: Fitted clear oak; 10 in./256 mm.; stamped in gold
Eagle/FABERGÉ/St. Petersburg/Moscow London.
ACC. NO. FAB66010

The tall silver-gilt vase is enamelled a translucent
white, the rim pierced and decorated with six stylized
cornflowers in green and blue *plique-à-jour* enamel.

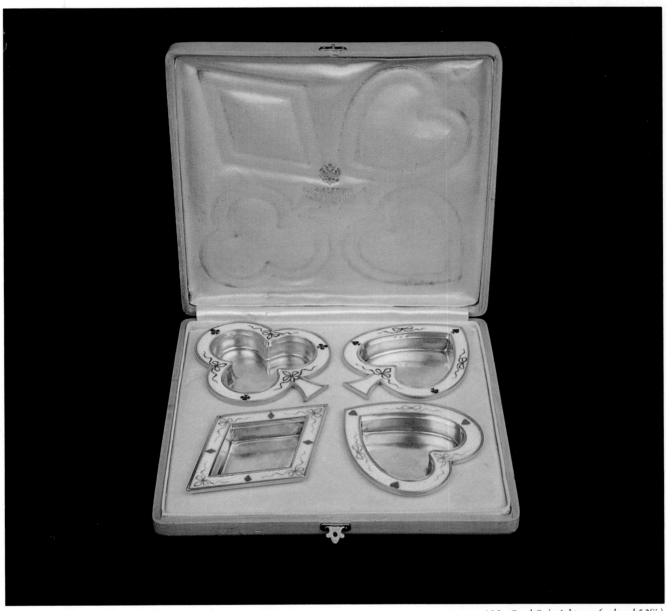

135. Card-Suit Ashtrays (reduced 52%)

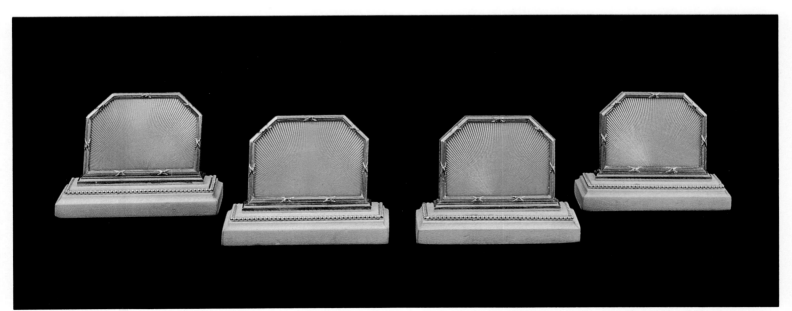

136. Four Menu Holders (reduced 45%)

103

COMPETITORS

Fabergé had many competitors, some worthy some not. This section has represented in it only two—selected because of the appeal of the objects rather than because the pieces were works representative of the *oeuvre* of particular firms. The triptych commemorating the three hundredth anniversary of Romanov rule is perhaps the most splendid and successful still extant piece in the Fabergé style created by the firm of Karl Hahn. It is quintessential Hahn in its slightly greater dependence on precious stones than is typical of comparable pieces by Fabergé. The presentation plaque by Ovchinnikov, on the other hand, is not a typical product of that firm. Their forte was pieces in the Pan-Slavic style. In that field their work is probably equal to, if not better than, Fabergé's chief supplier of the genre, the workshops of Fedor Rückert. The other major firms catering to the Pan-Slavic Market were those of Grachev Brothers and Ivan Petrovitch Klebnikov. More information on these and other firms working in this mode can be found in Marvin Ross' *The Art of Carl Fabergé and His Contemporaries*, Norman, Oklahoma, 1965.

In addition to that of Karl Karlovitch Hahn, some other houses which specialized in objects in the Western taste similar to those produced by Fabergé were Beilin, K. Bok and I. Britzin, all of whom worked for Fabergé before opening their own premises, and Bolin, Butz, Denissov, F. Kochli, Kortman, F.A. Lorié, I. Marshak, Morozov, Nichols and Plinke, and Rummer.

137. Samara Plaque (reduced 56%)

137. SAMARA PLAQUE, Ovchinnikov

14-1/4in./362mm.
MARKS: *anchors 84, EK, Eagle P. OVCHINNIKOV* lower front.
ACC. NO. FAB76019

A silver-gilt and enamel presentation plaque depicting a paddle steamer on a river by a town within a drapery border held aloft by a putto, the drapery inscribed in Cyrillic, *Samara and its Surroundings*, surmounted by the Russian Imperial Eagle within a black enamel shield, with blue enamel scrolling foliage mantel, also applied with another coat-of-arms and the date 1891. The border applied at each corner with the Russian Imperial Eagle inscribed at the top in Cyrillic *To His Imperial Highness, Heir to the throne and Grand Duke, Nicholas Alexandrovitch*, and at the bottom, *From the Samara Town Society in Remembrance*. Fabric backing and easel support.

Samara, now called Kuybyshev, is a large town some 200 miles south of Kasan on the Volga River.

Paul Akimovich Ovchinnikov and his son, Michael Pavelovskii, presided over the most successful Moscow firm of silversmiths and were in the vanguard of the Pan-Slavic movement, a revival of traditional Russian decorative forms, motifs and techniques. By 1872 the firm was granted a Royal Warrant (over a decade before the House of Fabergé was so honored), and in 1875 a branch was opened on the Morskaya in St. Petersburg.

The Samara Plaque is the product of an unknown workmaster EK (ЭК) of the St. Petersburg shop and in design reflects the more westernized taste of that city's clientele.

PROVENANCE
Presented to Czar Nicholas II by the Citizen's Society of the Town of Samara in 1891 while the former was still Czarevitch.
Anon. Sale: Sotheby Parke Bernet, New York, Lot 251, reproduced in catalogue.
A La Vieille Russie, New York.

138. ROMANOV TERCENTENARY TRIPTYCH, Hahn

5-1/2in./140mm.
6-3/4 in./172 mm. with easel.
MARKS: *HW, Eagle K. HAHN, 72 anchors* on triptych back; *Eagle K. HAHN, 72 anchors* on easel.
ACC. NO. FAB69005

It is of gold, the doors enamelled blue and applied with the crowned initials of Nicholas II and his wife, Alexandra Feodorovna, set with diamonds on white enamel cushions within diamond borders: the crowns are set with diamonds and two rubies. Above these are also applied gold plaques with the dates 1613 and 1913. The doors are opened by jewelled swing handles. The cresting is in the form of the Monamakh

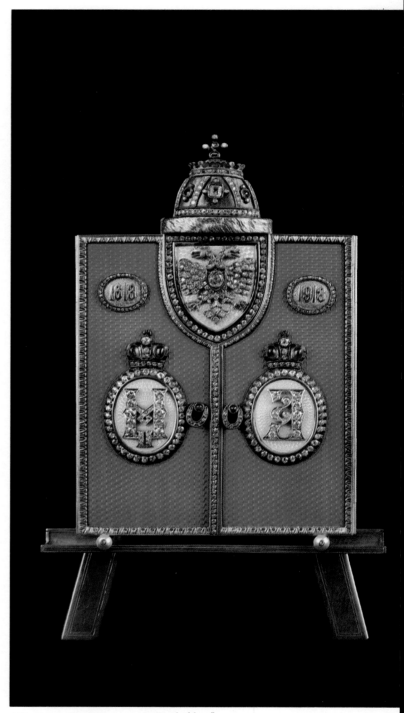

138. Romanov Tercentenary Triptych (closed)

crown or 'shapka,' which is applied with a diamond-set Imperial Eagle upon a white enamel cushion within a further diamond border. The doors curve about the eagle and open to reveal a white enamel panel applied with portraits of Nicholas II, Alexandra and Czarevitch Alexis, each within diamond-set borders and surmounted by crowns similar to those on the doors. Finally, there are diamond-set foliage sprays and the words in Russian "God be with us" also in diamonds. The reverse of the doors are engine-turned with sunbursts radiating from two discs engraved with the dates 1613 and 1913.

A crown is represented over each portrait and cypher. The 'shapka' of the cresting is the old Russian ducal

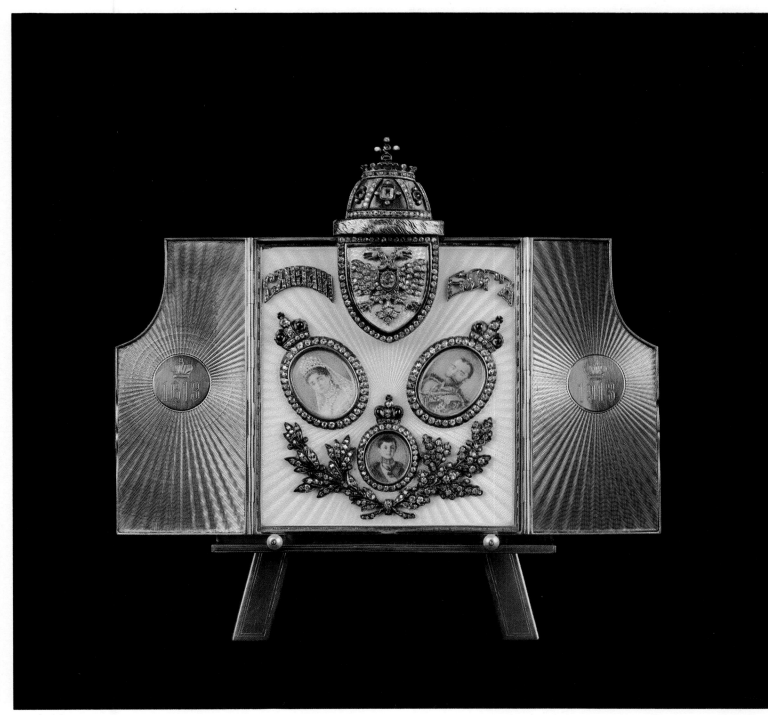

(open)

coronet allegedly worn by Vladimir Monamakh, the Viking who founded the first Russian dynasty in the ninth century. The dynasty came to an end early in the seventeenth century with Ivan the Terrible. A council elected Michael Romanov, grandfather of Peter the Great, as the next Czar and thus the Romanov dynasty was brought about. The Czar is shown in the uniform of His Imperial Majesty's Life Guard Hussar Regiment and the Czarevitch in that of the Foot Guards. The triptych was made to celebrate the Tercentenary of the Romanov dynasty of the Russian throne. Karl Karlovitch Hahn was Fabergé's closest rival and was also granted a Royal Warrant. His most important commission was for the diadem worn by the Czarina at her coronation.

(Appendix D for easel).

PROVENANCE

Czar Nicholas II.

Mrs. L. D. Hirst-Broadhead (Sale: Sotheby & Co., London, December 8, 1969, Lot 117, catalogue p. 49, reproduced both opened and closed in color opposite).

EXHIBITIONS

"A Loan Exhibition of the Works of Carl Fabergé," Wartski, London, 1949, no. 201, catalogue p. 19.

NYCC/Waterfield 1973, no. 50, catalogue pp. 106-7, reproduced in color twice.

REFERENCE

Art at Auction 1969-70, New York and London, 1970, p. 405, reproduced in color.

PACKING CASES

The packing cases fitted for the objects produced by the House of Fabergé are in themselves works of art. Most frequently made of hollywood, with white metal trefoil hinge clasps, some cases were made of birch and oak. These are most frequently found with earlier pieces. The interiors are shaped to accommodate the object and lined with off-white velvet. The lids are lined with white silk and stamped in gold or black ink with the mark of the house. These stamps vary and may in some cases be of use in dating or in identifying the city of manufacture of unstamped pieces. For example, cases made for pieces after the outbreak of the 1914 war are stamped *Petrograd* rather than the more German *St. Petersburg*. Boxes for pieces made in Moscow have that city's name stamped above or to the left of St. Petersburg. Cases for more important pieces, such as the Imperial Eggs, often were covered in velvet on the exterior.

Among the makers of the cases, Snowman (1964, pp. 125-6) lists three Finns, Käki and Kämäva and Otto Saikkonen, as well as an Estonian, Alfred Maripou.

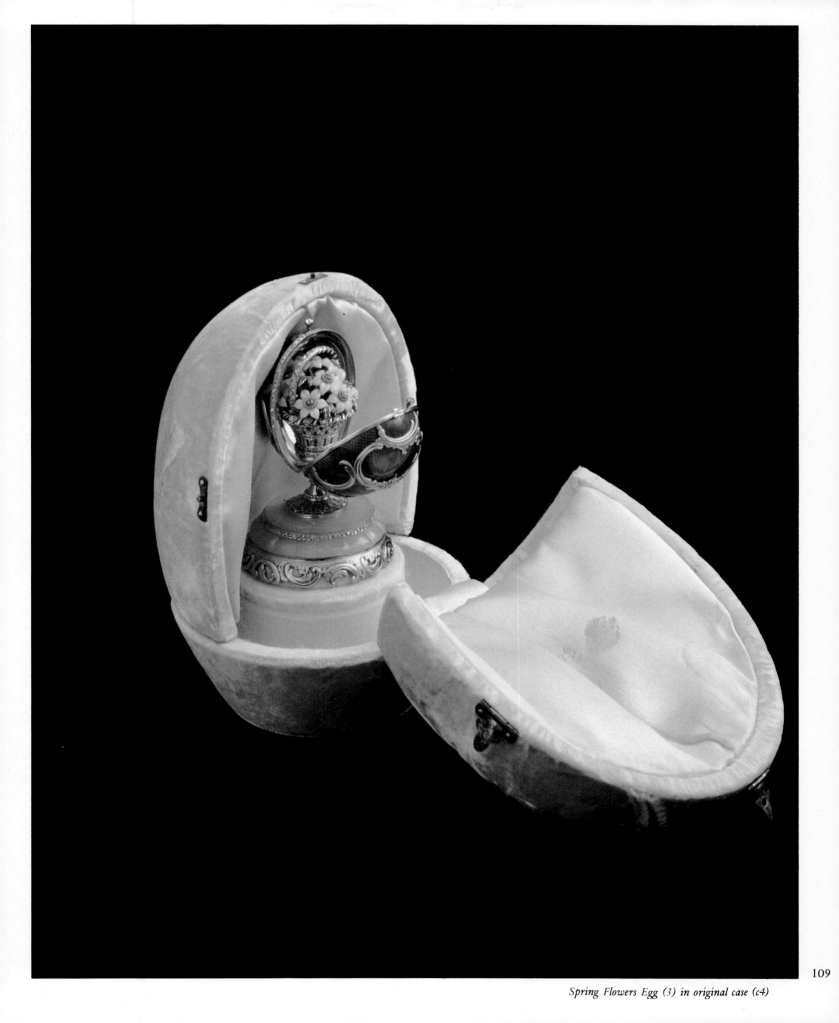

Spring Flowers Egg (3) in original case (c4)

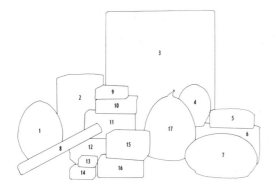

1. CROSS OF ST. GEORGE EGG (8)

Original fitted velvet-covered egg shape.
7-1/4 in./184 mm.
Stamped in gold *Eagle* (wings stylized to form a circle around other wording) */K. FABERGÉ/Petrograd Moscow/ Odessa London.*

2. DUCHESS OF MARLBOROUGH EGG (9)

Original fitted hollywood.
10 in./255 mm.
Stamped in black *Eagle/FABERGÉ/S. Petersburg/Moscow Odessa.*

3. IMPERIAL PRESENTATION FRAME (69)

Original fitted hollywood, lid applied with white metal Imperial Crown. Zippered pale green velvet slip-cover.
19 in./480 mm.
Stamped in gold *Eagle/K. FABERGÉ/St. Petersburg/Moscow.*

4. SPRING FLOWERS EGG (3)

Original fitted velvet-covered egg shape.
5-3/8 in./138 mm.
Stamped in gold *Eagle/FABERGÉ/St. Petersburg/Moscow London.*

5. CORONATION BOX (61)

Fitted green morocco, lid applied with gilt-metal Imperial Eagle.
5-1/4 in./133 mm.
Unstamped.

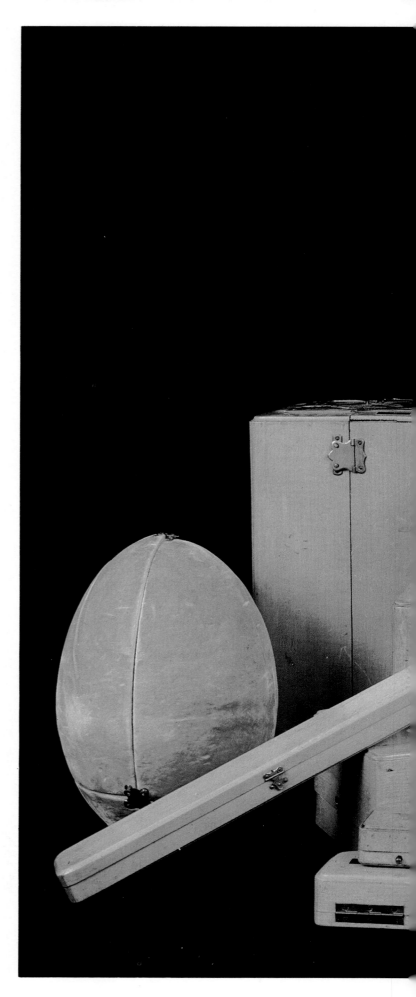

6. CORNFLOWER VASE (134)

Fitted clear oak.
10 in./256 mm.
Stamped in gold *Eagle/FABERGÉ/St. Petersburg/Moscow London.*

7. RENAISSANCE EGG (4)

Original fitted velvet-covered egg shape.
8 in./203 mm.
Stamp in gold obscured.

8. GRAND DUCHESS OLGA PAPER KNIFE (109)

Original fitted hollywood.
10 in./250 mm.
Stamped in black *Eagle/FABERGÉ/St. Petersburg/Moscow Odessa.*

9. SQUARE BOWENITE DISH (128)

Original fitted hollywood.
4 in./102 mm.
Stamped in black *Eagle/FABERGÉ/St. Petersburg/Moscow London.*

10. NICHOLAS II NEPHRITE BOX (63)

Original fitted hollywood.
7-1/8 in./181 mm.
Stamped in black *Eagle/FABERGÉ/Petrograd/Moscow London.*

11. WATERING CAN (56)

Original fitted hollywood.
4-7/8 in./120 mm.
Stamped in gold *Eagle/K. FABERGÉ/St. Petersburg/Moscow.*

12. STYLE-MODERNE KOVSH (126)

Original fitted hollywood.
6 in./153 mm.
Stamped in black *Eagle/St. Petersburg/Moscow London.*

13. VINAIGRETTE (68)

Original fitted hollywood.
2 in./45 mm.
Stamped in gold *Eagle/K. FABERGÉ/Moscow/S. Petersburg Odessa.*

14. PINK RABBIT (54)

Original fitted hollywood.
2-5/8 in./63 mm.
Stamped in gold *Eagle/FABERGÉ/St. Petersburg/Moscow.*

15. KELCH HEN EGG (10)

Original fitted hollywood.
4-1/2 in./107 mm.
Stamped in gold *Eagle/FABERGÉ/St. Petersburg/Moscow.*

16. FIRE-SCREEN FRAME (71)

Original fitted hollywood.
8 in./125 mm.
Stamped in black *Eagle/FABERGÉ/Petrograd/Moscow Odessa.*

17. FIFTEENTH ANNIVERSARY EGG (6)

Original fitted velvet-covered egg shape.
8-3/8 in./213 mm.
Stamped in black *Eagle/FABERGÉ/St. Petersburg/ Moscow London*

IMPERIAL EGGS

A CATALOGUE RAISONNÉ

A list illustrated with original drawings by B. Robert Shapiro of all the known Fabergé eggs presented by Czars Alexander III and Nicholas II to Czarinas Maria Feodorovna and Alexandra Feodorovna, including present whereabouts, sizes in inches and millimeters where known, and workmasters, if marked. For eggs bearing dates or commemorating specific anniversaries, the years are italicized. The sequence of the remaining eggs is largely conjecture.

In fact, the year in which the First Egg was presented cannot be fixed with any certainty. A. Kenneth Snowman makes a strong case for 1884 in his major reference work on Fabergé. H.C. Bainbridge, who worked for Fabergé for several years, however, points out in his book on the subject (Bainbridge 1966, pp. 123-24):

> As there is some doubt about this year (1884) — and as Perchin did not begin working for Fabergé until 1886, it is far more likely that the first egg was not made until 1886.

That all the eggs made prior to Perchin's death in 1903, for which the marks are known, bear his stamp further supports this idea. However, until evidence documenting one year or another comes to light, the date of the First Egg remains conjectural. The major difference in accepting 1884 as the date of the presen-

tation of the First Egg rather than 1886 is that two more eggs would have to be accounted for.

The circumstances surrounding the creation of the First Egg are also based on speculation. Whether the ingenious Fabergé sought Imperial favor by creating an egg to remind the Czarina of one she had seen in her native Denmark or whether the Czar approached Fabergé for an inspired Easter present after seeing the firm's gold-medal-winning *objets* at the Pan-Russian Exhibition in 1882 will probably never be known for sure. However, that so powerful a personality as Maria Feodorovna should have needed cheering up after the death of her hated, German-loving, commoner-marrying, son-and-heir-snubbing father-in-law is perhaps the least acceptable raison d'etre for the First Egg.

Whether the Imperial Warrant was the result of the First Egg's success or the Eggs resulted from Fabergé's obligation as a warrant holder to create a piece especially for the Czar, also awaits the unearthing of documentary evidence. The years 1884-86 were exceedingly important for the House of Fabergé and frustratingly, are poorly documented. In any case, by 1886, an Imperial Easter custom was begun that was to result in the creation of some of the most brilliant *chef d'oeuvres* of the goldsmith and jeweller's art.

ABBREVIATIONS

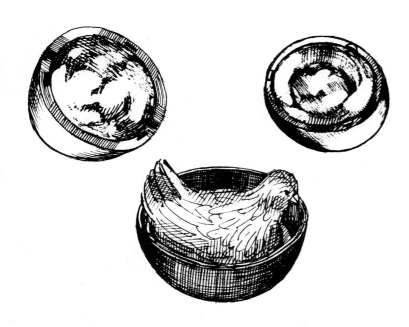

1886
FIRST IMPERIAL EGG

—

2-1/2 in./64 mm.
Forbes

1887
RESURRECTION EGG
Perchin
3-7/8 in./98 mm.
Forbes

1888

DANISH JUBILEE
EGG

1889

EGG WITH
BLUE ENAMEL RIBBING

Perchin
4-1/4 in./110 mm.
Stavros Niarchos, Paris

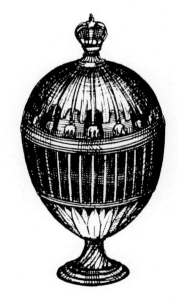

1890

SPRING FLOWERS
EGG

Perchin
3-1/4 in./83 mm.
Forbes

1891

AZOVA EGG

Perchin

3-7/8 in./98 mm.

Kremlin

1892

SILVER
ANNIVERSARY EGG

Perchin

3-1/4 in./83 mm.

Post

1893

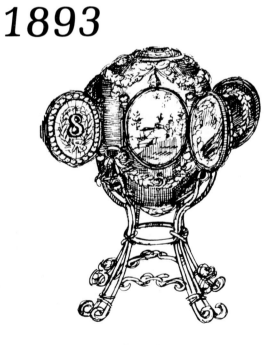

CAUCASUS EGG

Perchin

3-5/8 in./92 mm.

Gray

1894

RENAISSANCE
EGG

Perchin

5-1/4 in./140 mm.

Forbes

1895

(Alexandra)
ROSEBUD EGG

———

3 in./76 mm.

———

1895

(Maria)
DANISH PALACE EGG

Perchin

4 in./102 mm.

Gray

1896

(Alexandra)
EGG WITH REVOLVING MINIATURES

Perchin

10 in./154 mm.

Virginia

1896

(Maria)
BLUE SERPENT CLOCK EGG

Perchin

7-1/4 in./185 mm.

Private Collection, Switzerland

1897

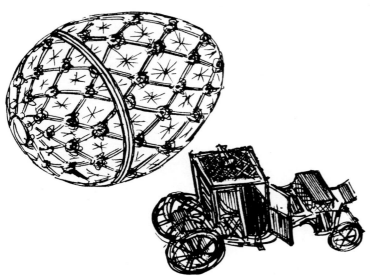

(Alexandra)
CORONATION EGG
Perchin
5 in./127 mm.
Wartski, London

1897

(Maria)
PELICAN EGG
Perchin
4 in./102 mm.
Virginia

1898

(Alexandra)

1898

(Maria)
LILIES OF
THE VALLEY EGG
Perchin
5-15/16in./267 mm.
Wartski, London

1899

(Alexandra)
MADONNA-LILY EGG
Perchin
10-1/2 in./267 mm.
Kremlin

1899

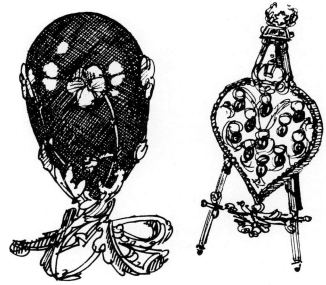

(Maria)
PANSY EGG
Perchin
5-3/4 in./146 mm.
Private Collection, U.S.A.

1900

(Alexandra)
CUCKOO EGG
Perchin
8-1/8 in./206 mm.
Mr. and Mrs. Bernard S.
Soloman, Los Angeles

1900

(Maria)
PINE CONE EGG
Perchin
3-3/4 in./95 mm.
Private Collection, U.S.A.

1901

(Alexandra)
TRANS SIBERIAN RAILWAY EGG
Perchin
10-3/4 in./273 mm.
Kremlin

1901

(Maria)
APPLE BLOSSOM EGG
Perchin
4-3/8 in./110 mm.
Private Collection, U.S.A.

1902

(Alexandra)
CLOVER EGG
Perchin
3-3/8 in./85 mm.
Kremlin

1902

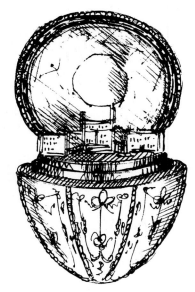

(Maria)
GATCHINA PALACE EGG
Perchin
5 in./127 mm.
Walters

1903

(Alexandra)
PETER THE GREAT EGG

Perchin

4-1/4 in./110 mm.

Virginia

1903

(Maria)
CHANTICLEER EGG

Perchin

12-5/8 in./320 mm.

Forbes

1904

(Alexandra)
USPENSKY CATHEDRAL EGG

—

14-1/2 in./370 mm.

Kremlin

1904

(Maria)
ALEXANDER III COMMEMORATIVE EGG

—

3-3/4 in./95 mm.

—

1905

(Alexandra)
COLONNADE EGG
Wigström
11-1/4 in./285 mm.
Royal Collection, England

1905

(Maria)

1906

(Alexandra)
SWAN EGG

4 in./102 mm.
Heirs of the late Maurice
Sandoz, Switzerland

1906

(Maria)

1907

(Alexandra)
ROSE TRELLIS
EGG
Wigström
3-1/16 in./77 mm.
Walters

1907

(Maria)

1908

(Alexandra)
ALEXANDER
PALACE EGG
Wigström
4-1/4 in./110 mm.
Kremlin

1908

(Maria)
PEACOCK EGG
Wigström
6 in./152 mm.
Heirs of the late Maurice
Sandoz, Switzerland

123

1909

(Alexandra)
STANDART EGG
Wigström
6-1/8 in./155 mm.
Kremlin

1909

(Maria)
—————

1910

(Alexandra)
EGG WITH
LOVE TROPHIES
—
Private Collection, U.S.A.

1910

(Maria)
ALEXANDER III
EQUESTRIAN EGG
—
6-1/8 in./155 mm.
Kremlin

1911

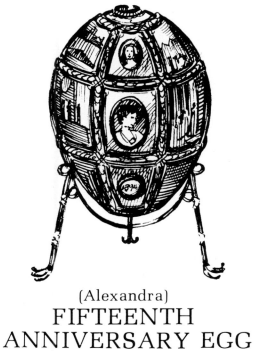

(Alexandra)
FIFTEENTH
ANNIVERSARY EGG

—

5-1/8 in./132 mm.

Forbes

1911

(Maria)
ORANGE TREE
EGG

—

10-1/2 in./267 mm.

Forbes

1912

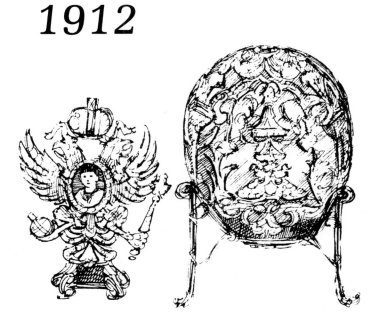

(Alexandra)
CZAREVITCH
EGG

Wigström

5 in./127 mm.

Virginia

1912

(Maria)
NAPOLEONIC
EGG

Wigström

4-5/8 in./117 mm.

Gray

1913

(Alexandra)
ROMANOV
TERCENTENARY EGG
Wigström
7-5/16 in./185 mm.
Kremlin

1913

(Maria)
WINTER EGG
—
4 in./102 mm.
Bryan Ledbrook, Esq.

1914

(Alexandra)
MOSAIC EGG
—
3-5/8 in./92 mm.
Royal Collection, England

1914

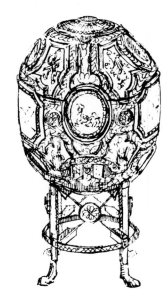

(Maria)
GRISAILLE EGG
Wigström
4-3/4 in./120 mm.
Post

1915

(Alexandra)
RED CROSS EGG
WITH RESURRECTION
TRIPTYCH

Wigström

3-3/8 in./85 mm.

Cleveland

1915

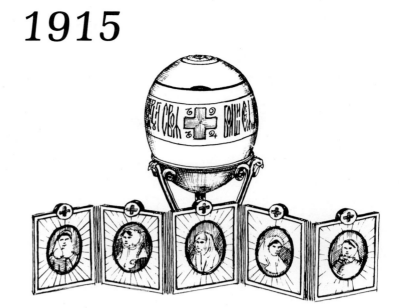

(Maria)
RED CROSS EGG
WITH PORTRAITS

Wigström

3-1/2 in./88 mm.

Virginia

1916

(Alexandra)
STEEL MILITARY EGG

Wigström

4 in./102 mm.

Kremlin

1916

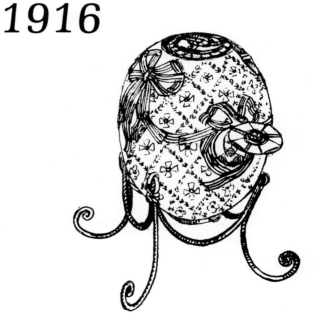

(Maria)
CROSS OF
ST. GEORGE EGG

3-5/16 in./90 mm.

Forbes

FABERGÉ COLLECTIONS
OPEN TO THE PUBLIC

Color television coverage and beautifully printed color blocks have made it possible for more and more people to enjoy the enchanted world of Fabergé. No matter how brilliant the photograph or creative the video presentation, however, there is no substitute for actually seeing the pieces themselves. In addition to the FORBES Magazine Collection which is on view in the lobby of the FORBES Building, 60 Fifth Avenue, New York, New York 10011 on business days from 9:00 a.m. to 5:00 p.m. and catalogued herein, a number of collections may also be viewed regularly. The annotated list of collections which follows will, it is hoped, be of help to those who wish to enjoy Fabergé firsthand.

In the United States

VIRGINIA MUSEUM OF FINE ARTS

Boulevard and Grove Avenue, Richmond, Virginia 23221
Tel. (804) 257-0844
Tuesday through Saturday 11:00 a.m. to 5:00 p.m.; Sunday 1:00 p.m. to 5:00 p.m.; closed Monday.

This is the most extensive public collection of Fabergé in the world. Assembled by Lillian Thomas Pratt and bequeathed to the museum upon her death in 1947, the collection includes five Imperial Eggs: the Egg with Revolving Miniatures (1896), the Pelican Egg (1898), Peter the Great Egg (1903), Czarevitch Egg (1912), and the Red Cross Egg with Portraits (1915). In addition there is a large selection of hardstone animals, miniature eggs, frames, handles, icons and jewelry as well as other Russian objets d'art of the period.

CATALOGUE: Parker Lesley, *Fabergé*, Richmond, Virginia, 1976. 160 pages. Over 300 color illustrations. Objects presented by type. Fully illustrated with every object reproduced in color. Excellent reproductions.

THE HILLWOOD COLLECTION

4155 Linnean Avenue, N.W., Washington, D.C. 20008
Tel. (202) 686-5807
Tours everyday except Tuesday and Sunday at 9:00 a.m., 10:30 a.m., 12:00 p.m. and 1:30 p.m. Advance registration required.

The Russian collection of the late Mrs. Marjorie Merriweather Post is beautifully displayed in the Georgian-style Washington mansion she built in the 1950s. Fabergé is just one aspect of the collection on view. Two Imperial Eggs, the Silver Anniversary Egg (1892) and the Grisaille Egg (1914), as well as an important selection of works in the Pan-Slavic style are among the highlights.

CATALOGUE: Marvin C. Ross, *The Art of Karl Fabergé and his Contemporaries*, Norman, Oklahoma, 1965. 238 pages. 75 color illustrations. Objects presented by workmaster. Scholarly text, graphically unsatisfactory. Especially good for information on Fabergé's competitors.

THE CLEVELAND MUSEUM OF ART

11150 East Boulevard, Cleveland, Ohio 44106
Tel. (216) 421-7340
Tuesday through Friday 10:00 a.m. to 6:00 p.m.; Saturday 9:00 a.m. to 5:00 p.m.; Sunday 1:00 p.m. to 6:00 p.m.; closed Monday.

The collection in the Cleveland Museum was assembled and left to the museum by the late India Early Minshall. A representative selection of Fabergé's work as well as that of some of his competitors, the collection includes, among other objects, one Imperial Egg, the Red Cross Egg with Resurrection Triptych (1915), several lovely flowers, some miniature furniture and a covered pot produced as part of the war effort.

CATALOGUE: Henry Hawley, *Fabergé and His Contemporaries*, Cleveland, Ohio, 1967. 139 pages. 7 color illustrations. Objects presented by workmaster and city of origin. All pieces illustrated, several good color blocks, informative text.

THE WALTERS ART GALLERY

600 North Charles Street, Baltimore, Maryland 21201
Tel. (301) 547-9000
Monday 1:00 p.m. to 5:00 p.m.; Tuesday through Saturday 11:00 a.m. to 5:00 p.m.; Sunday 2:00 p.m. to 5:00 p.m.

Parasol handles bought as presents by Henry Walters for his daughters when his yacht stopped at St. Petersburg, some hardstone animals and two Imperial Eggs, the Gatchina Palace Egg (1903) and the Rose Trellis Egg (1907) are the extent of the museum's holdings. The pieces are displayed with works by Lalique and other French *belle époque* jewellers. The contrast makes clear that Fabergé's genius lay in technique and tradition rather than in revolutionary design.

CATALOGUE: None. The Gatchina Palace Egg was reproduced in color in *Du* magazine, December 1977, p. 50, and both eggs are reproduced in black and white in Snowman 1962/64.

THE MATILDA GEDDINGS GRAY FOUNDATION COLLECTION

The collection is frequently on loan to museums throughout the United States.

Assembled by the late Matilda Geddings Gray of New Orleans, this collection is one of the most distinguished and sumptuous private collections in the United States. It boasts three Imperial Eggs: the Caucasus Egg (1893), the Danish Palace Egg (1895) and the Napoleonic Egg (1912), and the most important of Fabergé's exquisite flower pieces – the Basket of Lilies of the Valley, which was presented to Czarina Alexandra Feodorovna at the Nijegorodski Fair in 1896.

CATALOGUE: Susan Grady and William A. Fagaly, *Treasures by Peter Carl Fabergé and Other Master Jewellers*, New Orleans, 1972. Unpaginated. 11 color illustrations. Objects presented by type. The Gray Foundation Collection comprised over half of the objects featured in the National Geographic Society's 1977 exhibition "Objects of Fantasy: Peter Carl Fabergé and Other Master Jewelers" for which there is a modest catalogue.

In Europe

ARMORY MUSEUM

The Kremlin, Moscow
Tel. 22 67 847
A guide is required to enter the museum.

The Soviet government owns ten of Fabergé's Imperial Eggs: the Azova Egg (1891), the Madonna Lily Egg (1899), the Trans Siberian Railway Egg (1901), the Clover Egg (1902), the Uspensky Cathedral Egg (1904), the Alexander Palace Egg (1908), the Standart Egg (1909), the Alexander III Equestrian Egg (1910), the Romanov Tercentenary Egg (1913) and the Steel Military Egg (1916). The number of pieces on view varies and they are displayed by workmaster rather than as creations of the House of Fabergé.

CATALOGUE: I. Rodimseva, *Jewelled Objects of the Firm of Fabergé*, Moscow, 1971, 24 pages. 14 color illustrations. Objects presented by workmaster. Text in Russian. Color illustrations of eight of the eggs make this brochure worthwhile for those who may never get to Moscow.

THE WERNHER COLLECTION, LUTON HOO

Bedfordshire, England
Open to the public from Easter Saturday to the last Sunday in September.

The late Lady Zia Wernher was the daughter of Grand Duke Michael of Russia and the Countess Torby, who were patrons of Fabergé, and from whom Lady Zia inherited most of her Fabergé pieces. Additional show pieces bought by her husband, Sir Harold Wernher, including a magnificent nephrite tray and an important Imperial Presentation Box complete the collection. It is an interesting one in that, for the most part, it was assembled before the Russian Revolution, while the House of Fabergé was a going concern.

CATALOGUE: None. Two pages in the Luton Hoo brochure provide some background information and illustrations.

THE VICTORIA AND ALBERT MUSEUM

South Kensington, London S.W. 7, England
Tel. (01) 589-6371
Jewelry Gallery hours as of January 1979: Monday through Thursday, and Saturday, 10:00 a.m. to 6:00 p.m.; Sunday 2:30 p.m. to 6:00 p.m.; closed Friday.

The museum's major piece, the square gold enamel Imperial Presentation Box is supplemented by the generous loan from Wartski of two of the most well-known Imperial Eggs, the Coronation Egg (1897) and the Lilies of the Valley Egg (1898).

CATALOGUE: None. All three of these pieces are reproduced in color in Snowman 1962/64.

THE ROYAL COLLECTION AT SANDRINGHAM

Inquiries should be directed to Buckingham Palace.

The collection of Her Majesty Queen Elizabeth II is in numbers the largest holding of Fabergé's works in the world. King Edward VII and Queen Alexandra were leading patrons of the House of Fabergé, and for them the extensive series of Sandringham animals was made. Other animals, flowers and boxes were popular birthday, anniversary and Christmas presents. Queen Mary shared her parents-in-law's love of Fabergé and added to the collection two Imperial Eggs, the Colonnade Egg (1905) and the Mosaic Egg (1914), as well as one of the equally splendid Kelch Eggs.

CATALOGUE: None. Two hundred and seventy-five pieces from the Royal Collection at Sandringham formed the bulk of the major Fabergé retrospective held on the occasion of the Queen's Silver Jubilee in 1977. The catalogue (V & A/Snowman 1977) is the best source of information on the collection. Other members of the Royal Family including H.M. Queen Elizabeth, The Queen Mother, H.R.H. The Prince of Wales, H.R.H. The Princess Anne, H.R.H. The Princess Margaret, H.R.H. The Duke of Kent and H.R.H. The Duke of Gloucester all own pieces of Fabergé, many of which were also lent to the Jubilee exhibition and are included in the catalogue.

FABERGÉ REPRODUCED IN FORBES MAGAZINE

Since unveiling this collection on the Fiftieth Anniversary of FORBES Magazine in 1967, many of the pieces pictured in this catalogue have appeared in FORBES in beautiful color photographs by Feliciano and his mentor Howard Graff. A chronological list of these handsome reproductions is published here for the first time.

Issue date	Pg. no.	Object [s]	Cat. no. [s]
3/1/67	44	Renaissance Egg	4
5/1/67	62	Fifteenth Anniversary Egg	6
5/15/67	62	Spring Flowers Egg	3
6/15/67	70	Orange Tree Egg	7
8/1/67	40	Chanticleer Egg	5
9/1/67	65	Crystal Polar Bear	52
3/1/68	37	Duchess of Marlborough Egg	9
3/15/68	74	Imperial Presentation Frame	69
5/1/68	67	Kelch Hen Egg	10
6/15/68	52	Dancing Moujik	49
8/1/68	37	Rabbit Egg	11
10/1/68	65	Perpetual Desk Calendar	111
		Oval Bell Push	105
		Serpent Pen	110
2/1/69	46	Egg Bonbonnière	13
3/15/69	72	Sedan Chair	58
5/15/69	226	Chapka Egg	sold
7/1/69	51	Nicholas II Nephrite Box	63
8/15/69	73	Basket of Lilies of the Valley	60
		Watering Can	56
10/15/69	54	Coronation Box	61
12/15/69	54	Nephrite Hen Egg	sold
2/15/70	46	Louis XVI Snuffbox, *Blerzy*	65
		Louis XVI-Style Snuffbox	66
4/15/70	62	Gueridon	59
6/1/70	41	Thirty-two Miniature Easter Eggs	15-48
8/1/70	32	Eagle Vase	120
10/1/70	60	Purpurine Tray	sold
1/15/71	34	Miniature Coin Tankard	119
3/15/71	58	Twenty-Fifth Anniversary Clock	102
5/1/71	38	Oval Rhodonite Dish	127
7/15/71	54	Book Marker	112
		Magnifying Glass	114
		Nephrite Paper Knife	113
9/1/72	34	Hoof Egg	12
4/1/72	47	Ostrich-Feather Fan	85
		Lorgnette	90
6/15/72	64	Cornflower Vase	134
		Egg Scent Flaçon	14
		Square Bowenite Dish	128
8/15/72	72	Gold Presentation Cigarette Case	64
10/1/72	64	Owl Seal	55
		Style-Moderne Kovsh	126
		Circular Pink Agate Dish	130
12/1/72	75	Pair of Vodka Cups	121
		Art Nouveau Match-Holder	133
3/15/73	96	Spring Flowers Egg	3
7/15/73	76	Kelch Hen Egg	10
9/15/73	115	Lattice-Work Frame	73
3/15/74	69	Fire-Screen Frame	71
6/1/74	54	Imperial Parasol Handle	86
8/1/74	43	Knitting Needles	92
9/15/74	114	Pen Rest	107
		Silver and Leather Desk Pad	sold
6/1/75	55	Captain of the 4th Harkovsky Lancers	50
8/15/75	58	Rock Crystal Frame	72
2/1/76	64	Helmet Cup	122
10/1/76	112	Pink Handle	88
		Festooned Fan	93
12/1/76	94	Large Silver Kovsh	117
2/1/77	74	Cross of St. George Egg	8
5/1/77	102	Round Bowenite Dish	121
		Card Holder	107
		Grand Duchess Olga Paper Knife	109
3/1/77	81	Large Hollywood Frame	84
		Carelian Birch Frame	83
12/15/77	80	Card Suit Ashtrays	135
2/6/78	77	Amatory Frame	76
5/29/78	97	Oval Bell Push	105
		Round Bell Push	104
10/16/78	174	Imperial Cylinder Vase	125

FABERGÉ TO SEE AND BUY

Great and historic pieces make rare appearances on the market. However, the firm catered to such a large and international clientele during its heyday that many beautifully worked pieces of all types and descriptions can still be found — and bought — for ever larger sums of money. There are two major firms which always have in stock a selection of precious bibelots from the House of Fabergé. These are A La Vieille Russie run by the Schaffer Family in New York and Wartski headed by A. Kenneth Snowman in London. The list below begins with these two *grands specialistes* followed alphabetically by other firms which also usually have pieces on display.

A LA VIEILLE RUSSIE
781 Fifth Avenue, New York, New York 10022
Tel. (21) 752-1727

WARTSKI
14 Grafton Street, London W1X 3LA, England
Tel. (01) 493-1141-2-3

ASPREY & COMPANY LIMITED
165-169 New Bond Street, London W1Y OAR, England
Tel. (01) 493-6767

BENTLEY & CO.
65, New Bond Street, London W1, England
Tel. (01) 629-0651

DAVID ORGELL
320 North Rodeo Drive, Beverly Hills, CA. 90210
Tel. (213) 275-2081 or (213) 272-4550

JAN SKALA
1 West 47th Street, New York, New York 10036
Tel. (212) CI6-2814

In addition, the great auction houses usually have one or two major Russian sales every season in which are included works by Fabergé. In recent years the most important sales have been held by Christie's in Geneva and Sotheby Parke Bernet in New York.

CHRISTIE, MANSON & WOODS INTERNATIONAL, INC.
502 Park Avenue, New York, New York 10022
Tel. (212) 826-2828

CHRISTIE'S (INTERNATIONAL) S.A.
8 Place de la Taconnerie, 1204 Geneva, Switzerland
Tel. 28 25 24

CHRISTIE, MANSON & WOODS, LTD.
8 King Street, St. James's, London, SW1Y 6QT, England
Tel. (01) 839-9060

SOTHEBY PARKE BERNET, INC.
980 Madison Avenue, New York, New York 10021
Tel. (212) 472-3400

SOTHEBY PARKE BERNET & CO.
34-35 New Bond Street, London W1A 2AA, England
Tel. (01) 493-8080

SOTHEBY PARKE BERNET MONACO S.A.
Sporting D'Hiver, Place du Casino, Monte Carlo, Monaco
Tel. (93) 30-8880

SOTHEBY PARKE BERNET A.G.
20 Bleicherweg, CH-8022 Zürich, Switzerland
Tel. (1) 202 00 11

Pieces also frequently appear at:

PHILLIPS
867 Madison Avenue, New York, New York 10021
Tel. (212) 734-8330

PHILLIPS, SON & NEALE
Blenstock House, 7 Blenheim Street, New Bond Street, London W1Y OAS, England
Tel. (01) 629-6602

MES. ADER PICARD TAJAN
12, Rue Favart, 75002 Paris, France
Tel. 742-95-77

KOLLER GALERIE
Rämistrasse 8, 8001 Zürich, Switzerland
Tel. 01-475040

WILLIAM DOYLE GALLERIES
175 East 87th Street, New York, New York 10028
Tel. (212) 427-2730

PLAZA ART GALLERIES, INC.
406 East 79th Street, New York, New York 10021
Tel. (212) 472-1000

C.C. SLOAN & COMPANY, INC.
715 Thirteenth Street, N.W. Washington, D.C. 20005
Tel. (202) 628-1468

ROBERT C. ELDRED CO., INC.
Box 796, East Dennis, Massachusetts 02641
Tel. (617) 385-3116

COLLECTIONS PAST

The changes of ownership of works of art, their so-called "provenance," is a fascinating study in itself. Fabergé was fashionable among the rich and powerful before 1917 and since the fall of the Romanovs and the dissolution of the firm, it has become increasingly sought after by succeeding generations of collectors. Among those who have owned one or another of the pieces illustrated in this volume are such diverse notables as J.P. Morgan, President Franklin Roosevelt and King Farouk.

The list which follows begins with the Russian Imperial Family and then alphabetically gives the names of collectors, title and catalogue number of objects owned, and, where warranted, additional information on the collection.

IMPERIAL FAMILY
First Imperial Egg (1), Resurrection Egg (2), Spring Flowers Egg (3), Renaissance Egg (4), Chanticleer Egg (5), Fifteenth Anniversary Egg (6), Orange Tree Egg (7), Cross of St. George (8), Pink Rabbit (54), Silver Presentation Paddle Steamer (57), Basket of Lilies of the Valley (60), Coronation Box (61), Blue Rocaille Box (62), Nicholas II Nephrite Box (63), Gold Presentation Cigarette Case (64), Louis XVI Snuffbox, *Blerzy* (65), Louis XVI-Style Snuffbox (66), Imperial Presentation Frame (69), Heart Surprise Frame (70), Marie Pavlovna Mirror (74), Carelian Birch Frame (83), Imperial Parasol Handle (86), Admiral Grand Duke Alexis Cuff Links (98), Presentation Document Holder (101), Hvidore Seal (103), Grand Duchess Olga Paper Knife (109), Samara Plaque, *Ovchinnikov* (137), Romanov Tercentenary Triptych, *Hahn* (138).

MME. ELIZABETH BALLETTA
OF THE IMPERIAL MICHAEL THEATER
The leading ballerina of the sunset years of Imperial Russia, Mme. Balletta was the mistress of both Nicholas II and his uncle, Grand Duke Alexander. She was presented with many beautiful pieces including the famous Balletta Box. Much of her collection was acquired by Lansdell K. Christie. See Christie reference.

Watering Can (56).

HERR BOMM, VIENNA
Coronation Box (61).

ARTHUR E. BRADSHAW
Orange Tree Egg (7), Coronation Box (61).

BRANDEIS UNIVERSITY
Silver Presentation Paddle Steamer (57).

MR. & MRS. C. J. BYRNE
Twenty-Fifth Anniversary Clock (102).

MRS. R. L. CAMERON
Four Menu Holders (136).

MRS. ISABELLA CATT
Oval Rhodonite Dish (127).

T. H. CHING, NEW YORK
Hat Pin (95).

MRS. HUGH J. CHISHOLM, JR.
Card-Suit Ashtrays (135).

LANSDELL K. CHRISTIE, LONG ISLAND
Mr. Christie's was the largest private collection of Fabergé in the United States prior to his death in the mid 1960s. Numbering almost two hundred pieces, it was exhibited at the Metropolitan Museum from 1962 to 1966. See Corcoran 1961, *Great Private Collections*/Snowman, and *Metropolitan Bulletin*/McNab Dennis.

Spring Flowers Egg (3), Chanticleer Egg (5), Kelch Hen Egg (10), Rabbit Egg (11), Egg Scent Flaçon (14), Miniature Eggs (15-27), Dancing Moujik (49), Crystal Polar Bear (52), Watering Can (56), Basket of Lilies of the Valley (60), Coronation Box (61), Nicholas II Nephrite Box (63), Louis XVI Snuffbox, *Blerzy* (65), Louis XVI-Style Snuffbox (66), Fire-Screen (71), Frame Pink Whistle (87), Miniature Nephrite Kovsh (131).

H. T. DE VERE CLIFTON
Clifton also owned the Rosebud Egg of 1896, now listed as whereabouts unknown. One story has it that the egg was destroyed when hurled across the room during a domestic dispute.

Renaissance Egg (4).

ZENAS MARSHAL CRANE OF CRANE PAPER AND DESCENDANTS
Large Silver Kovsh (117).

MAJOR W. HEAFORD DAUBNEY
Daubney's was a collection of over two dozen *objets*. See the 1949 Wartski exhibition catalogue and the catalogue for Christie's, London, November 14, 1961, Lots 162-178. Several of the lots are illustrated.

Vodka Cup with Sapphires (121).

LADY LYDIA DETERDING, PARIS
Heart Surprise Frame (70).

RICHARD R. DRAPER, ST. LOUIS
Badge of the Brotherhood of the Holy Ghost of the Trinity (94), Cornflower Vase (134).

THE DVANI FAMILY, GEORGIA, RUSSIA
Large Silver Kovsh (117).

H. M. KING FAROUK
The last Egyptian monarch was a great enthusiast of Fabergé. His extensive collection, which also included the Swan Egg, was sold by order of the Egyptian government. See the catalogue for Sotheby & Co., Cairo, March 10-13, 17-20, 1954, Lots 101-166, 630-636, 1209-1217. Several lots are illustrated.

Kelch Hen Egg (10), Book Blade and Loop (115), Vodka Cup with Sapphires (121).

LADY GRANTCHESTER
First Imperial Egg (1), Resurrection Egg (2).

MRS. L. D. HIRST-BROADHEAD
Mrs. Hirst-Broadhead's extensive Russian collection included over twenty-five pieces of Fabergé. See the catalogue for Sotheby & Co., London, December 8, 1969, Lots 90-91, 98-111, 114-116, 118-126. Several of the lots are illustrated including eight in color.

Lorgnette (90), Book Marker (112), Nephrite Paper Knife (113), Magnifying Glass (114), Romanov Tercentenary Triptych, *Hahn* (138).

A. G. HUGHES, ENGLAND
Orange Tree Egg (7).

MRS. J. M. JACQUES, ENGLAND
Nicholas II Nephrite Box (63).

MILDRED KAPLAN, NEW YORK
Orange Tree Egg (7).

BARBARA BAZANOV KELCH
Mrs. Kelch was one of the richest women in Russia. Using her money, her husband Alexander was able to compete with the Czar in the elaborateness of his Easter presentation eggs. In addition to the Hen Egg, Snowman lists three others: the Egg with Twelve Panels, the Rocaille Egg, and the Bonbonnière Easter Egg.

Kelch Hen Egg (10).

MR. & MRS. JACK LINSKY, NEW YORK
The other major piece in this collection was the Rocaille Egg presented by Alexander Kelch to his wife in 1902. See Kelch reference.

Renaissance Egg (4), Sedan Chair (58).

W. MAGALOW
Orange Tree Egg (7).

THE DUCHESS OF MARLBOROUGH, BLENHEIM PALACE
Duchess of Marlborough Egg (9).

J. P. MORGAN, NEW YORK
Sedan Chair (58).

ELLIOTT ROOSEVELT, NEW YORK
Silver Presentation Paddle Steamer (57).

FRANKLIN D. ROOSEVELT, "TOP COTTAGE," HYDE PARK, NEW YORK
Silver Presentation Paddle Steamer (57).

MAURICE SANDOZ, SWITZERLAND
The chemical magnate's collection in Switzerland was one of the most important in Europe. The family still owns the Swan Egg, the Peacock Egg and the Youssoupoff Egg. The latter was presented to Princess Zenaide Youssoupoff by her husband, Prince Felix, on the occasion of their twenty-fifth wedding anniversary. The egg's three small frames originally contained portraits of Prince Felix and his sons, Felix and Nicholas, but these were later replaced by cameo monograms of the letter S (Sandoz). The younger Prince Felix was one of the assassins of Rasputin. See Snowman 1962/64. Several pieces are illustrated, but not attributed.

Chanticleer Egg (5), Orange Tree Egg (7), Imperial Presentation Frame (69), Fire-Screen Frame (71).

PETER OTWAY SMITHERS, M.P.
Smithers' was a collection of over thirty works including many enamelled *objets de luxe* and desk pieces. See the 1949 Wartski exhibition catalogue.

Ostrich-Feather Fan (85).

ROBERT STRAUSS, STONEHURST, ENGLAND
This important collection was especially strong in hard-stone animals and flowers. See catalogue for Christie's, May 9, 1976, Lots 1-58. All of the pieces are illustrated in color.

Book Blade and Loop (115).

MRS. L. TURNBULL, ENGLAND
Egg Bonbonnière (13).

MME. GANNA WALSKA
Duchess of Marlborough Egg (9).

CHARLES WARD, PRESIDENT OF BROWN AND BIGELOW
Silver Presentation Paddle Steamer (57).

ANNA LOIS WEBBER
Miniature Eggs (35, 37).

WORKMASTERS
THEIR MARKS AND THEIR WORK

Peter Carl Fabergé employed some of the most talented jewellers, goldsmiths, artists and designers of the period. Under his guiding genius these diverse artistic personalities worked together to create the marvelous *objets* to which this book is devoted. Directly below Fabergé himself, in the firm's heirarchy, were the so-called workmasters. These individuals, who in several cases had their own firms which were merged into the Fabergé establishment, presided over teams of craftsmen. Directed by the workmasters, the workshops often specialized in one aspect of the entire firm's diverse output. For example, August Wilhelm Holmström specialized in jewelry, Julius Alexandrovitch Rappoport produced table and decorative silver and the independent workshops of Fedor Rückert executed many pieces in the Pan-Slavic or Old Russian style. The two most renowned workmasters of all, Michael Perchin and Henrik Wigström, are famous for the legendary Imperial Eggs as well as other works of fantasy.

The list which follows begins with these two men and then, alphabetically, their colleagues. Provided for all are biographical data, marks in Roman letters (and Cyrillic where applicable—many workmasters used only Roman initials) and an index of the works produced by them which are illustrated in this volume. An alphabetical list of other workmasters terminates this appendix.

MICHAEL EVLAMPIEVITCH PERCHIN. The only one of Fabergé's leading workmasters of Russian origin, Perchin was born in Petrozavodsk in 1860 and died in 1903. Despite very humble origins he was so talented as to be established as head of his own workshop by the age of 26. All the marked Imperial Eggs made prior to his death are the work of Perchin's shop.

MARK: MP/МП

WORKS ILLUSTRATED: Resurrection Egg (2), Spring Flowers Egg (3), Renaissance Egg (4), Chanticleer Egg (5), Duchess of Marlborough Egg (9), Kelch Hen Egg (10), Rabbit Egg (11), Hoof Egg (12) Miniature Eggs (33?, 36, 45), Sedan Chair (58), Basket of Lilies of the Valley (60), Blue Rocaille Box (62), Louis XVI-Style Snuff-Box (66), Circular Bonbonnière (67), Imperial Presentation Frame (69), Crystal Frame (72), Amatory Frame (76), Pink Oval Frame (77), White Frame (78), Laurel-Sprig Frame (80), Pink Rocaille Opera Glasses (89), Presentation Document Holder (101), Hvidøre Seal (103), Round Bell Push (104), Card Holder (106), Pen Rest (107), Serpent Pen (110), Perpetual Desk Calendar (111), Book Marker (112), Book Blade and Loop (115), Pair of Vodka Cups (121), Round Bowenite Dish (129), Striated Agate Kovsh (132).

HENRIK WIGSTRÖM. The man who succeeded Perchin was a Swedish Finn from Ekenäs. Born in 1862, he survived the House of Fabergé by about a dozen years. All the Imperial Eggs made after 1903 known to bear initials are the work of Wigström; however, only about half are stamped. In addition to several of the great eggs, many of the hardstone figures were assembled in Wigström's workshop.

MARK: HW

WORKS ILLUSTRATED: Egg Bonbonnière (13), Egg Scent Flaçon (14), Miniature Eggs (28, 29, 38, 42), Captain of the 4th Harkovsky Lancers (50), Owl Seal (55), Silver Presentation Paddle Steamer (57), Nicholas II Nephrite Box (63), Fire-Screen Frame (71), Ostrich-Feather Fan (85), Knitting Needles (92), Festooned Fan (93), Pink-Egg Cuff Links (100), Twenty-Fifth Anniversary Clock (102), Magnifying Glass (114), Imperial Cylinder Vase (125), Square Bowenite Dish (128), Circular Pink Agate Dish (130), Art Nouveau Match-Holder (133).

JOHAN VICTOR AARNE. Aarne returned to his native Finland in 1891 to become a workmaster in Tampere before being hired by Fabergé that same year. His workshop produced gold and silver objects many of which were translucently enamelled in the Western taste. Eventually Aarne returned to Viipuri, Finland, where he was born in 1863, and established his own firm there. He was succeeded by Armfelt.

MARK: BA, occasionally JVA

WORKS ILLUSTRATED: Miniature Eggs (26, 27), Lattice-Work Frame (73), Marie Pavlovna Mirror (74), Pink Handle (88), Decanter Stopper (124).

FEDOR AFANASSIEV. Like Perchin a native of Russia, Afanassiev specialized in small objects of fantasy.

MARK: FA/ФА)

WORKS ILLUSTRATED: Miniature Eggs (16, 48), Pair of Angel Fish (53), Oval Rhodonite Dish (127).

KARL GUSTAV HJALMAR ARMFELT. Aarne's successor was a Swedish Finn born in Hango. He was first apprenticed to Paul Fredrik Sohlman before coming to the House of Fabergé, where he specialized in small enamelled objects of gold and silver. He left the firm during the war.

MARK: JA/ЯА)

WORK ILLUSTRATED: Vieux-Rose Frame (79).

AUGUST FREDERICK HOLLMING. Another Finn, born in Loppis in 1854, Hollming specialized in stone objects and small gold and silver enamelled pieces. After his death in 1915, he was succeeded by his son Väino. One of his descendants continues the family's lapidary interest in Germany.

MARK: A*H

WORKS ILLUSTRATED: Miniature Eggs (31?, 44), Crystal Polar Bear (52), Admiral Grand Duke Alexis Cuff Links (98).

AUGUST WILHELM HOLMSTRÖM. Until his death in 1903, Holmström worked as Fabergé's chief jeweller. A Swedish Finn, he was born in Helsingfors, in 1829, and was succeeded by his adoptive son Albert.

MARK: AH

WORK ILLUSTRATED: Coronation Box (61).

ERIK KOLLIN. A specialist in gold objects, most notably the award-winning replicas of the Scythian gold found in Kerch, Kollin was a Swedish Finn born in Pojo in 1836. After an apprenticeship at Ekenäs and the under Holmström, he opened his own workshop in 1870, the year Carl Fabergé took over control of his father's firm.

MARK: EK

WORKS ILLUSTRATED: Miniature Eggs (19, 30), Miniature Coin Tankard (119).

G. LUNDELL. The man who followed Brockman as workshop manager in Odessa, Lundell was a Swedish Finn, specializing in small conventional articles, who worked first in St. Petersburg.

MARK: GL/ Г Л

WORK ILLUSTRATED: Miniature Egg (16).

ANDERS JOHAN NEVALAINEN. Nevalainen became a Fabergé workmaster in 1885, after an apprenticeship in Holmström's workshop. A Finn, born in Pielisjärvi in 1858, he made articles such as frames and boxes for St. Petersburg and Moscow as well as for export to London.

MARK: AN

WORKS ILLUSTRATED: Pale Blue Frame (75), Kaiser Wilhelm II Frame (81), Double Agate Frame (82), Carelian Birch Frame (83), Four Menu Holders (136).

GABRIEL NIUKKANEN. Another Finn, who made small conventional articles in gold and silver.

MARK: GN

WORK ILLUSTRATED: Gold Presentation Cigarette Case (64).

J. F. OKERBLOM. A member of an important family of Russian silversmiths working in the nineteenth century.

MARK: IO

WORK ILLUSTRATED: Miniature Egg (22), which bears the mark IO. If not Okerblom, then an unrecorded workmaster of the period.

KNUT OSKAR PIHL. Holmström's nephew by marriage, Pihl was also a specialist in jewelry and jewelled objects. A Swedish Finn from Pojo, Pihl died in 1897 at the age of thirty. His son also worked at Fabergé's with Holmström père and fils, and after the revolution, was employed by Tillander in Finland.

MARK: OP

WORK ILLUSTRATED: Miniature Egg (34).

JULIUS ALEXANDROVITCH RAPPOPORT. Rappoport was the principal silversmith of the House of Fabergé. His work is of good quality but otherwise unexceptional. He was born in Germany in 1864, arrived in St. Petersburg when he was nineteen. He set up his own workshop shortly thereafter.

MARK: IP

WORK ILLUSTRATED: Badge of the Brotherhood of the Holy Ghost of the Trinity (94).

WILHELM REIMER. A specialist in small gold objects and jewelry, Reimer was born in Pernau.

MARK: WR

WORK ILLUSTRATED: Miniature Egg (47?).

ALFRED THIELEMANN. A specialist in jewelry and jewelled objects, Thielemann was a Russian of German parentage. After his death c. 1908, he was succeeded by his son, Karl Rudolph Thielemann.

MARK: AT

WORKS ILLUSTRATED: Miniature Eggs (35, 37, 41?) Eagle Vase (120).

ALEXANDER TILLANDER. An independent workmaster of considerable skill, Tillander worked most frequently for the House of Hahn, Fabergé's principal rival. He is said to have been murdered by his own workers during the revolution.

MARK: AT/⟨AT⟩

WORK ILLUSTRATED: Miniature Egg (23).

WORKMASTER HH. A Fabergé jeweller previously unrecorded.

MARK: HH

WORK ILLUSTRATED: Set of Five Buttons (91).

OTHER WORKMASTERS

(not represented in this volume)

ANDREJ GORIANOV. Gorianov was a maker of jewelry and small accessories who succeeded Reimer.

MARK: AG/АГ

ANDERS MICHELSSON. Michelsson was a maker of jewelry and occasional fantasy pieces. A Swedish Finn born in Pytis in 1839, he succeeded Ringe in St. Petersburg jointly with Soloviev.

MARK: AM

PHILIP THEODORE RINGE. Like his successors Michelsson and Soloviev, a maker of jewelry, boxes and fantasy pieces, Ringe was a German working in St. Petersburg.

MARK: TR

FEDOR RÜCKERT. A Moscow silversmith specializing in the Pan-Slavic style, Rückert did not work exclusively for Fabergé, and his was probably the most important of the independent workshops to receive regular commissions from the firm.

MARK: FR/ФР

EDWARD WILHELM SCHRAMM. Another St. Petersburg-based German, Schramm made jewelry and other small conventional pieces.

MARK: ES

VLADIMIR SOLOVIEV. A specialist in small enamelled pieces, Soloviev was a Russian who with Michelsson succeeded Ringe in St. Petersburg.

MARK: BC

STEPHAN WÄKEVÄ. A maker of conventional table and display silver, Wäkevä was born in Säckjärvi, Finland in 1833. He was succeeded by his son Alexander.

MARK: SW

ADDITIONAL INFORMATION

The most important source of information, not only on Fabergé workmasers, but also lapidaries, branch managers and others associated with the House of Fabergé is A. Kenneth Snowman's, *The Art of Carl Fabergé.* The 1962 and 1964 editions have more information than the 1953 edition.

DETAILS & COMPARISONS

When viewing works produced by the House of Fabergé, one is often so engrossed with the ensemble, that the details are overlooked or forgotten. The photographs in this appendix highlight a wide range of details from stands to struts to miniatures to matrixes. In most cases, they picture portions of objects hidden or not clearly visible in the color plates. In other instances, the photographs portray earlier objets from which Fabergé may have derived inspiration or other pieces by Fabergé similar to those in this book. For the Chanticleer Egg, not only are details reproduced, but also a period photograph showing the Egg in the process of creation. It is hoped that these details and comparisons will prove enlightening.

HEART SURPRISE FRAME (70)

DUCHESS OF MARLBOROUGH EGG (9)

Inscribed *K. FABERGÉ* in Cyrillic.

Foot inscribed *K. FABERGÉ 1902.*

CHANTICLEER EGG (5)

Back showing covered key holes.

Shell removed to reveal mechanism.

Silver key.

A.K. Snowman Collection

Original Fabergé photograph showing egg near completion (detail).

KELCH HEN EGG (10)

Egg and hen opened, miniature easel folded.

Egg closed.

Substitute miniature (tinted photograph) of Nicholas II.

Cleveland Museum of Art

India Early Minshall Lapis-Lazuli Egg, opened.

ORANGE TREE EGG (7)

Howard Graff

Egg unopened.

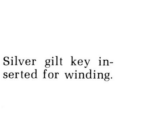

Silver gilt key inserted for winding.

Chased gold grillwork concealing mechanism.

Sotheby Parke Bernet

Richard of Paris, Orange Tree with Singing Bird, 27 in./700mm.

RENAISSANCE EGG (4)

Grünes Gelwolbe, Dresden

Leroy of Amsterdam, Egg Casket in chalcedony, 5½ in./140mm.

DUCHESS OF MARLBOROUGH EGG (9)

Wartski

Back showing winding knob.

Imperial Serpent Clock Egg.

SEDAN CHAIR (58)

Poles detached, door opened to show interior.

HELMET CUP (122)

Resting on finial as a cup.

LORGNETTE (90)

Second lense folded under.

PINK HANDLE (88)

Mounted as a letter knife with blade by Scott.

NEPHRITE DESK PAD (108)

Hidden pencil removed.

HOLY GHOST BADGE (94)

Back showing Cyrillic inscription: *Emblem of the Vilna Brotherhood of the Holy Ghost of the Trinity 1909.*

FIVE BUTTONS (91)

"Hairpin" back.

ADMIRAL LINKS (98)

Chain catch, attached and detached.

TREFOIL AND CROWN LINKS (97 & 99)

"Propellor" backs, opened and closed.

139

HVIDØRE SEAL (103)

Matrix inscribed
Hvidøre.

HELMET SEAL (51)

Matrix cut with prancing horse.

The widowed Denmark sisters, Czarina Maria Feodorovna and Queen Alexandra at Hvidøre in 1913.

CROSS OF ST. GEORGE EGG (8)

Chased silver monogram of Dowager Empress Maria Feodorovna.

Date chased in silver.

FIFTEENTH ANNIVERSARY EGG (6)

Cypher of Czarina Alexandra Feodorovna under finial table diamond with chased gold palmette surround.

Czar Nicholas II
(b. 1868)

Czarina Alexandra
(b. 1872)

Czarevitch Alexis
(b. 1904)

Bottom table diamond with chased gold palmette surround.

Grand Duchess Olga
(b. 1895)

Grand Duchess Tatiana
(b. 1897)

Grand Duchess Marie
(b. 1899)

Grand Duchess Anastasia
(b. 1901)

Ovals painted with dates, and signatures, in Cyrillic, *FA/BER/GE* hidden in festooned garlands.

The Alexander III Museum.

The opening of the Alexander III bridge in Paris.

The Huis ten Bosch, the Hague.

The procession to Uspensky Cathedral.

The moment of Coronation.

The reception for the members of the First State Duma, the Winter Palace, St. Petersburg.

The unveiling of the monument commemorating the Bicentenary of the Battle of Poltava.

The unveiling of the statue of Peter the Great at Riga.

The removal of the remains of the Saint Serafim Sarovski.

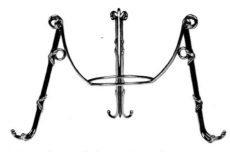

Original stand for Fifteenth Anniversary Egg (6).

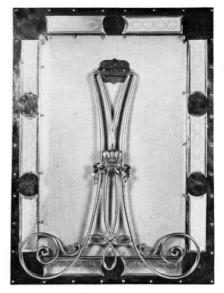

Imperial Presentation Frame mounted with crown (69).

Original stand for the Cross of St. George Egg (8).

Kelch Hen Egg (10) stand, made for King Farouk.

Perpetual Desk Calendar (111)

Original easel for Romanov Tercentenary Triptych by Hahn (138).

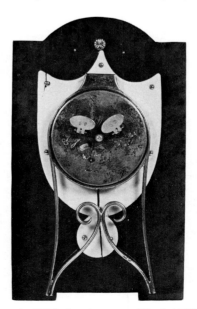

Twenty-Fifth Anniversary Clock (102)

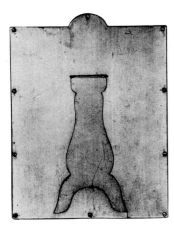

Pale Blue Frame (75)

Rock Crystal Frame (72)

Lattice-Work Frame (73)

White Frame (78)

Amatory Frame (76)

Pink Oval Frame (77)

Laurel-Sprig Frame (80)

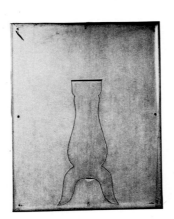

Marie Pavlovna Mirror (74)

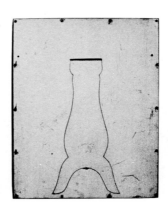

Kaiser Wilhelm II Frame (81)

Hollywood Frame (84)

Carelian Birch Frame (83)

143